UNEP

GLOBAL GENDER AND ENVIRONMENT OUTLOOK

The Critical Issues

SWEDEN

Network of Women
Ministers and Leaders
for the Environment

UN
WOMEN

WECF
International

UNDP
Empowered lives.
Resilient nations.

RIO+
WORLD CENTRE
FOR SUSTAINABLE
DEVELOPMENT

UNITED NATIONS
UNIVERSITY

UNU-EHS
Institute for Environment
and Human Security

UNITED NATIONS
UNIVERSITY

UNU-GEST
Gender Equality Studies
and Training Programme

UNIVERSITY OF ICELAND

Welcome to the *Global Gender and Environment Outlook The Critical Issues*. The authors and the UNEP Secretariat provide in this assessment an overview of critical evaluations and analyses of the interlinkages between gender and the environment, and their importance for gender-sensitive policy-making and actions.

The Global Gender and Environment Outlook (GGEO) was first proposed by the Network of Women Ministers and Leaders for the Environment (NWMLE) to UNEP at the United Nations Conference on Sustainable Development (Rio+20). The 2014 United Nations Environment Assembly subsequently welcomed the development of the GGEO, and the use of social science information and gender relevant indicators to examine the links between gender and the environment (UNEP GC Decision 27/11).

The GGEO provides an overview of existing knowledge to generate insights and propose some answers to the following key policy-relevant questions:

- What social forces are producing the changes seen in the environment, and are they gender dependent?

- What are the large-scale consequences of ongoing ecological changes for social systems and human security, and are the impacts gender-differentiated?

- What do future projections and outlooks look like, are they gender-differentiated, and will there be different outcomes for women and men?

- What actions could be taken for a more sustainable future that will position women and men as equal agents in taking such actions, and which socio-economic factors will shape different outcomes and responses for women and men?

The GGEO has been developed and written by a global team of almost 50 experts, with inputs from major groups and international organizations. We wish to thank all those who have contributed to the GGEO and look forward to the uptake of its findings at the second United Nations Environment Assembly (UNEA-2) in Nairobi in May 2016.

GGEO The Critical Issues is an abridged version prepared specifically for UNEA-2 of the comprehensive GGEO. The full report will be available later in 2016.

Foreword

Virtually everywhere in the world, environmental change has different impacts on women and men. Gender also has a role in determining how – and sometimes whether – people are able to act as agents of change on their own natural environments.

Perhaps recognizing this reality, the poet Maya Angelou has called on us "to recognize and celebrate our heroes and she-roes". For me, these include people such as Rachel Carson, the author of *Silent Spring*, and Professor Wangari Maathai, who founded the Greenbelt movement in Kenya. It also includes the villagers in India who started the Chipko movement against deforestation, as well as the many people around the world who are protesting environmental degradation and the effects of climate change.

At the 2012 United Nations Conference on Sustainable Development (Rio+20), UNEP, in response to a request from the Network of Women Ministers and Leaders for Environment, committed to undertake a global assessment of the environment, focusing on gender. The result – which reflects the joint efforts of UNEP, UN Women and other partners – is the *Global Gender and Environment Outlook* (GGEO) report, the first comprehensive global assessment of the gender-and-environment nexus.

The GGEO report is essential reading for those interested in the social dimensions of environmental issues. For readers who want to better understand current environmental challenges, and for those seeking innovative and effective solutions, the report describes policy options and concrete opportunities to contribute to the future we want: a future of justice and equality that leaves no one behind. It reflects and builds on the groundbreaking work of hundreds of scientists, policy experts, gender advocates and members of community groups. And it examines a wide range of topics, including food production, water and sanitation, energy, sustainable consumption and production, fisheries and fishing communities, and forests and those who depend on them for their livelihoods.

The 2030 Agenda for Sustainable Development highlights the close links between gender and environment, and between gender and sustainable development more broadly. By working to eliminate gender inequalities in communities and societies around the world, we can open up new environmental solutions, and we can go a long way toward realizing all 17 Sustainable Development Goals.

There has already been progress on many fronts. The importance of the gender-and-environment nexus has been acknowledged in several international agreements and many national policies. Analyses of gender-environment links are driving efforts such as the development of cleaner-burning cookstoves and more equitable water distribution schemes. The number of Global Environment Facility projects that take gender into account has more than doubled following the organization's adoption of a gender-mainstreaming plan.

But there is still a long way to go before both gender equality and a healthy environment are realized around the globe. The GGEO report represents an important step toward the development of more sustainable, just and equitable people-and-environment policies.

Achim Steiner

United Nations Under-Secretary-General and
Executive Director, United Nations Environment Programme

Acronyms and Abbreviations

ASM	artisanal and small-scale mining
BAU	business-as-usual
BPA	bisphenol-A
BRS	the Basel, Rotterdam and Stockholm Conventions
CBD	United Nations Convention on Biological Diversity
CDKN	Climate and Development Knowledge Network
CEDAW	United Nations Convention on the Elimination of All Forms of Discrimination Against Women
CIFOR	Center for International Forestry Research
CO_2	carbon dioxide
COP	conference of the parties
DALY	deaths and disability-adjusted life years
DCPI	Division of Communication and Public Information (UNEP)
DDE	dichlorodiphenyldichloroethylene
DDT	dichlorodiphenyltrichloroethane
DEPI	Division of Environmental Policies and Implementation (UNEP)
DESA	Department of Economic and Social Affairs (UN)
DEWA	Division of Early Warning and Assessment (UNEP)
DPSIR	drivers, pressures, states, impacts, responses
DRR	disaster risk reduction
DTIE	Division of Technology, Industry and Economics (UNEP)

ENERGIA	International Network on Gender and Sustainable Energy
EU	European Union
FAO	Food and Agriculture Organization of the United Nations
FUGs	forest user groups
GACC	Global Alliance for Clean Cookstoves
GBV	gender-based violence
GDP	gross domestic product
GGCA	Global Gender and Climate Alliance
GIAs	gender impact assessments
GLAAS	Global Analysis and Assessment of Sanitation and Drinking Water (UN-Water)
GM	genetically modified
GSSU	Gender and Social Safeguards Unit (UNEP)
HAP	household air pollution
ICRW	International Center for Research on Women
IDRC	International Development Research Centre
IFPRI	International Food Policy Research Institute
IISD	International Institute for Sustainable Development
ILO	International Labour Organization
IMF	International Monetary Fund
INDCs	Intended Nationally Determined Contributions
IPCC	Intergovernmental Panel on Climate Change
IUCN	International Union for Conservation of Nature
IUU	illegal, unregulated and unreported (fishing)

LGBT	lesbian, gay, bisexual and transgender
MeHg	methyl mercury
MHM	menstrual hygiene management
NGO	non-governmental organization
NTFP	non-timber forest product
NWMLE	Network of Women Ministers and Leaders for the Environment
OECD	Organisation for Economic Co-operation and Development
PAHs	polycyclic aromatic hydrocarbons
PCBs	polychlorinated biphenyls
REDD/REDD+	United Nations collaborative initiative on Reducing Emissions from Deforestation and forest Degradation in developing countries
Rio+20	United Nations Conference on Sustainable Development, Rio de Janeiro, Brazil, 2012
SDGs	Sustainable Development Goals
SEI	Stockholm Environment Institute
SIDS	Small Island Developing States
SIGI	Social Institutions and Gender Index (OECD)
STEM	Science, Technology, Engineering and Mathematics
UAE	United Arab Emirates
UNCCD	United Nations Convention to Combat Desertification
UNCED	UN Conference for Environment and Development, Rio de Janeiro, Brazil, 1992
UNDP	United Nations Development Programme
UNEA-2	Second United Nations Environment Assembly
UNEP	United Nations Environment Programme

UNESCO	United Nations Educational, Scientific and Cultural Organization
UNFCCC	United Nations Framework Convention on Climate Change
UNICEF	United Nations Children's Emergency Fund
UNISDR	United Nations Office for Disaster Risk Reduction
UNON	United Nations Office at Nairobi
UNSD	United Nations Statistics Division
UNU	United Nations University
USA	United States of America
WASH	water, sanitation and hygiene
WECF	Women in Europe for a Common Future
WEF	World Economic Forum
WHO	World Health Organization
wPOWER	Partnership on Women's Entrepreneurship in Renewables
WWF	World Wildlife Fund
ZIKV	Zika virus

Acknowledgements

Coordinating Lead Author
Joni Seager, Bentley University, USA

Lead Authors
Jamie Bechtel, New Course, USA
Sabine Bock, WECF International, Germany
Irene Dankelman, Radboud University, the Netherlands
Maureen Fordham, Northumbria University, UK
Sascha Gabizon, WECF International, the Netherlands
Nguyen Thuy Trang, UNEP, Kenya
Leisa Perch, RIO+ Centre/UNDP, Brazil
Seemin Qayum, UN Women, USA
Ulrike Roehr, genanet, Germany
Tina Schoolmeester, GRID-Arendal, Norway
Joni Seager, Bentley University, USA
Rahel Steinbach, UNEP, France
Meriel Watts, Pesticide Action Network Asia and Pacific, New Zealand
Claudia Wendland, WECF International, Germany

Contributing Authors
Lorena Aguilar, IUCN, USA
Isis Alvarez, Global Forest Coalition, Colombia
Katia Araujo, Huairou Commission, USA
Josephine Bauer, UNEP, Kenya
Gillian Bowser, Colorado State University, USA
Alexandra Caterbow, WECF International, Germany
Cosmin Corendea, UNU, Germany
Anna Donners, Ministry of Foreign Affairs, the Netherlands
Soma Dutta, ENERGIA, India
Silja Halle, UNEP, Switzerland
Markus Ihalainen, CIFOR, Kenya
YuYun Ismawati, Indonesian Toxics-Free Network, Indonesia
Deepa Joshi, Wageningen University, the Netherlands
Lucia Kiwala, UN-HABITAT, Kenya
Lilja Kolbeinsdóttir, Ministry for Foreign Affairs of Iceland/ICEIDA, Mozambique
Barbara van Koppen, International Water Management Institute, South Africa
Tanya McGregor, Secretariat of the CBD, Canada

Ambinintsoa Lucie Noasilalaonomenjanahary, Ministry of Environment, Ecology, Sea and Forest, Madagascar
Rebecca Pearl-Martinez, Tufts University, USA
Cheney Shreve, Northumbria University, UK
Vivienne Solis Rivera, CoopeSoliDar, Costa Rica
Elena Villalobos Prats, WHO, Switzerland
Isabell Wienphal, WECF International, Germany

Science Editor
John Smith, USA

Reviewers
Belinda Abraham, UNICEF, Vietnam
Bina Agarwal, University of Manchester, UK
Sara Ahmed, IDRC, Canada
Haroon Akram-Lodhi, Trent University, Canada
Gotelind Alber, GenderCC-Women for Climate Justice, Germany
Bimbika Sijapati Basnett, CIFOR, Kenya
Leigh Brownhill, Athabasca University, Canada
Flavia Ciribello, UN Women Regional Office for Eastern and Southern Africa, Kenya
Garette Clark, UNEP, France
Peter Denton, Greenethics, Canada
Sarah Dickin, SEI, Sweden
Judith van Eijnatten, Pacific Community-SPC, the Netherlands
Madeleine Fogde, SEI, Sweden
Jennifer Francis, Asian Development Bank, Philippines
Wendy Harcourt, Erasmus University, the Netherlands
Corinne Hart, GACC, Washington, D.C.
Jason Jabbour, UNEP, USA
Alejandro Jimenez, SIWI, Sweden
Isabell Kempf, UNEP-UNDP PEI, Kenya
Matthias Kern, UNEP Secretariat of the BRS Conventions, Switzerland
Victoria Luque, UNEP-UNDP PEI, Kenya
Olimar Maisonet-Guzman, US Department of State, USA
Piedad Martín, UNEP, Panama
Chenje Munyaradzi, UNEP, Kenya
Joke Muylwijk, Gender and Water Alliance, the Netherlands
Esther Mwangi, CIFOR, Kenya
Michiko Okumura, UNEP, Kenya
Ana Rojas, IUCN, the Netherlands
Annadis Rudolfsdottir, University of Iceland, Iceland
Carolyn Sachs, Pennsylvania State University, USA

Kalpana Sharma, India
Beverly Stoeltje, Indiana University, USA
Jerker Tamelander, UNEP, Thailand
Annabell Waititu, IEWM, Kenya
Jaime Webbe, UNEP/UN-REDD, Kenya
Moa Westman, UNEP-UNDP PEI, Kenya

Data Specialist
Rebecca Pearl-Martinez, Tufts University, USA

Data Advisory Group
Bimbika Sijapati Basnett, CIFOR, Kenya
Thomas Brooks, IUCN, USA
Cheryl Doss, Yale University, USA
Molly Gilligan, IUCN, USA
Allie Glinski, International Centre for Research on Women, USA
Sarah Harper, University of British Columbia, Canada
Corinne Hart, GACC, USA
Caitlin Kieran, IFPRI, USA
Rachel Mahmud, GACC, USA
Sheila Oparaocha, ENERGIA, the Netherlands
Annette Prüss-Ustün, WHO, Switzerland
Kame Westerman, Conservation International, USA

Our thanks to many people who supported the work
Nurgul Asylbekova, UN Women, Ukraine
Nargis Azizova, UN Women, Kyrgyzstan
Farida Balbakova, Global and Local Information Partnership (GLIP), Kyrgyzstan
Marta Birna Baldursdóttir, University of Iceland, Iceland
Irma Erlingsdottir, University of Iceland, Iceland
Mbarou Gassama, UN Women, Senegal
Francesca Greco, UNESCO, Italy
Diane Husic, Moravian College, USA
Marie Jalabert, UNEP, France
Laura Jungman, RIO+ Centre/UNDP, Brazil
Rebekah Kading, Colorado State University, USA
Laura Kramer, State University of New York at Albany, USA
Cate Owren, IUCN, Gender Office, USA
Kristjana Þ Sigurbjörnsdóttir, University of Iceland, Iceland
Anke Stock, WECF International, Germany
Carolyn Vickers, WHO, Switzerland
Pennsylvania State University, USA: David Agole, Christy Beck, Kelsey Brain, Isaac Bretz, Sarah Eissler, Meredith Field, Alexander Fyfe, Elizabeth Garner, Anne Odele, Carolyn Reyes, Abou Traore

GGEO Community of Practice team
Sascha Gabizon, WECF International, the Netherlands
Johanna Hausmann, WECF International, Germany
Victor Nthusi, UNEP, Kenya
Evelyn Ongige, UNEP, Kenya

UNEP team
Overall coordination
Monika MacDevette, DEWA
Janet Kabeberi-Macharia, Gender and Social Safeguard Unit (GSSU)
Jacqueline McGlade, DEWA
Nguyen Thuy Trang, DEWA

Support team
Josephine Bauer, DEWA
Harsha Dave, DEWA
Winnie Gaitho, DEWA
Linda Kaseva, GSSU
Nyokabi Mwangi, DEWA
Pauline Mugo, DEWA
Ruth Mukundi, DEWA
Ruth Njoroge, GSSU
Hanul Oh, DEWA
Evelyn Ongige, DEWA
Kate Teperman, GSSU
Victor Tsang, GSSU
Damaris Waigwa, DEWA
Mick Wilson, DEWA

Communication, design and graphics
Amber Anderson, DCPI
Bálint Márton, Hungary
Kelvin Memia, DCPI
Martin Michuki, UNON Publishing Services Section
Jennifer Odallo, UNON Publishing Services Section
Hanul Oh, DEWA
Evelyn Ongige, DEWA
François Rogers, CatalySD Sustainability, UK
Jinita Shah, UNON Publishing Services Section
Kate Teperman, GSSU
Shereen Zorba, DCPI

Table of contents

Figures

Tables

Boxes

THE GENDER-AND-ENVIRONMENT NEXUS: TOWARDS MORE EQUITABLE AND INCLUSIVE FORMS OF SUSTAINABILITY

A moment of happiness, Nobel laureate Professor Wangari Maathai and former Swedish Environment Minister Lena Sommestad, after the 2004 Nobel Peace prize announced in Nairobi, Kenya.

Photo credit: © Franz Dejon

CHAPTER 1

Why the outlook on gender and the environment is needed

The Global Gender and Environment Outlook (GGEO) occupies a unique space in the landscape of global assessments, highlighting a new framework with which to look at social and economic development. The GGEO is not simply a matter of *'add women to the environment and stir'*; instead it makes use of gender-based assessment frameworks along with the traditional environmental assessment approach of the Drivers-Pressures-State-Impacts-Responses (DPSIR) methodology, thus requiring new questions and new methods.

Whether environmental change is acute, or slow and chronic, it has specific differentiated impacts on women and girls or on men and boys. Using a gender-specific approach to examine these complex linkages (which may be referred to as the "gender-and-environment nexus") is therefore an appropriate way to investigate the dynamic relationships between environmental change and gender equality, as well as between impacts on sustainablity and the realization of women's rights and empowerment (Leach 2015, Seager 2014).

Recognition of current environmental impacts is taking place at the same time that global policy and advocacy efforts aimed at gender equality (as well as equality with respect to class/income, race/ethnicity and other types of differences) are gaining traction. The push for gender equality is shaping environmental understanding, but notions of gender equality are also shaped by environmental imperatives including equal access to, and sharing of, the benefits of the use and protection of ecosystems and natural resources (UN 2014, MEA 2005).

Environmental feminist movements: stories of inspiration

There is a long history leading up to today's focus on the gender-and-environment nexus, including the path-breaking work of hundreds of scholars, practitioners, community groups and gender advocates. Rachel Carson's 1962 book, *Silent Spring*, brought the environmentally harmful impacts of indiscriminate pesticide use to public attention and called for immediate policy response. Her work, and that of others who were inspired by it, led to a ban on general use of DDT in the United States in 1972. *Silent Spring* has continued to inspire environmentalists and environmental movements.

In the 1970s some of the earliest ecofeminist writings constructed powerful narratives about women's deep connections to nature and the environment. The women's peace movements in the 1970s and 1980s synthesized concerns about sustainability, environmental protection, women's equality and environmental health. One of the best known of these was the Greenham Women's Peace Camp in the United Kingdom (1981-2000).

A number of powerful movements concerned with women and the environment have set the stage for more ambitious and deep-rooted transformational approaches. In India the Chipko movement to protect forests essential for community livelihoods against destructive logging began in 1973; the Indian scientist and environmental activist Vandana Shiva's work on food and agriculture, including food sovereignty and biodiversity conservation, is widely recognized. In Kenya the Green Belt Movement, launched by Nobel laureate Professor Wangari Maathai, has planted over 51 million trees in Kenya. These women and others are celebrated not only as symbols of women's environmental protest, but also for helping to broaden conceptions of the gender-and-environment nexus.

An impressive body of feminist theory, perspectives and initiatives has sharpened, enhanced and transformed environmental and sustainability analyses in different ways. The overall conclusion of this work is that the holistic nature of the gender-and-environment nexus requires:

• analysing the different dimensions of relationships between humans and the environment across geographic scales;

• establishing how environmental conditions shape the lives of women and men in different ways as a result of gender and other differentiators;

• developing frameworks and perspectives that allow an understanding that women and men are not only affected by, but also have important roles to play in enabling, environmental sustainability;

• demonstrating that ignoring these issues in environmental and climate policies and programmes, based on a belief in their gender neutrality, is a recipe for failure (Aguilar et al. 2015, Nightingale 2006).

The Chipko Movement in India Photo credit: © Anupam Mishra; Wangari Maathai, 2004 Nobel Peach laureate and founder of the Green Belt Movement Photo credit: © Joseph Sohm / Shutterstock.com; Vandana Shiva, food sovereignty and biodiversity activist Photo credit: © www.navdanya.org

International commitments to gender equality and sustainable development

During several decades of women's movements and activism, international agreements and commitments have evolved from being completely silent on the differential impacts of economic development on the environment and on women and men, to a situation today in which environment and gender equality are at the core of *Transforming our World: The 2030 Agenda for Sustainable Development* (UN 2015).

In 1979 the Convention on the Elimination of All Forms of Discrimination against Women (CEDAW) was adopted by the UN General Assembly to provide for the advancement of non-discrimination and human rights through the obligation of governments to promote, protect and fulfil the equal rights of men and women (UN 1979).

The 1995 Beijing Declaration and Platform for Action called for building on the progress made on environment and development at the UN Conference on Environment and Development (UNCED) in Rio de Janeiro in 1992, and for the full and equal participation of women and men as agents and beneficiaries of sustainable development (UN 1995).

The three Rio Conventions on biodiversity, desertification and climate change, resulting from the 1992 UN Conference on Environment and Development (UNCED), have incorporated gender concerns in varying ways:

- The preamble to the Convention on Biological Diversity (CBD) recognizes the vital role women play in the conservation and sustainable use of biodiversity. It promotes full participation by women at all levels of policy-making and implementation for biodiversity conservation activities.

- The UN Convention to Combat Desertification (UNCCD) has mainstreamed gender issues since its inception. Its prologue emphasizes the central role played by women in regions affected by desertification and/or drought, particularly in rural areas of developing countries, and the importance of ensuring full participation by both women and men at all levels in programmes to combat desertification and mitigate the effects of drought.

- The UN Framework Convention on Climate Change (UNFCCC) first addressed gender in 2001 at the seventh Conference of the Parties (COP7), when it mandated that national adaptation programmes of action be guided by gender equality. COP13 in Bali, Indonesia, in 2007 saw the launch of groups such as the Women for Climate Justice Network and the Global Gender and Climate Alliance. In late 2015 the UNFCCC Paris Agreement recognized the intersection of climate change and gender equality, empowerment of women and realization of their rights.

Gender was also addressed during the 2015 Conferences of the Parties to the Basel, Rotterdam and Stockholm Conventions. The main gender focus in these conventions is on the impact of poor management of hazardous chemicals and wastes on vulnerable groups, including women and young children. There is now greater recognition of the links between gender, poverty, and hazardous chemicals and wastes, as well as of the profound significance the gender/poverty nexus can have for both sensitivity and exposure over time – and thus on economic, social and environmental well-being.

In September 2015 world leaders committed to the 2030 Agenda for Sustainable Development, in which gender issues are not only mainstreamed but taken forward through a global push to create lasting change based on one simple principle: everything is connected. The 17 Sustainable Development Goals (SDGs) in the 2030 Agenda address human rights and well-being through a common understanding that a healthy environment is integral to the full enjoyment of basic human rights, including the rights to life, health, food, water and sanitation, and quality of life. Interwoven into this is the concept that by directly addressing the interlinkages between gender and the environment, new opportunities will open up to help achieve the SDGs in a more effective, sustainable and beneficial manner.

Overall, the level of engagement by the international community in the gender-and-environment nexus has significantly increased; the question remains, however, whether the 15 years of the 2030 Agenda will see greater gender equality in terms of access to natural resources, environmental livelihoods and a clean, healthy environment.

The need for gender-disaggregated information

One of the strongest messages emerging from the body of analyses and reports on the gender-and-environment nexus is the crucial need for gender-disaggregated data. In the absence of such data, environmental analyses remain inadequate and partial, and establishing baselines, monitoring progress and assessing outcomes is almost impossible.

Progress on reducing gender gaps is difficult to measure if the data only "count women" without deeper consideration of gender discrimination and power relations, which by excluding women (or men) from certain rights, privileges and institutions can result in an imbalance of numbers and data.

In practice, the term gender is still being used as a proxy for women with little or no analysis of the power relations between women and men within households and broadly in society, or of intersecting inequalities based on class/income, age, location, race/ethnicity and other characteristics (Harris 2011).

The consideration of gender, in both policy and practice, is generally couched in heteronormative terms such as the binary sex variable: male or female. "Gender is used as an umbrella term for two mutually exclusive and stable categories of men and women (and sometimes boys and girls), but most often refers euphemistically to women. ... Gender equality or inequality is most often presented as a comparative metric between the two sexes with little reference to structural origins or relations of power and domination" (Razavi and Qayum 2015).

Inequality and gaps in gender inclusion

Inequality globally is greater today than at any time since the 1950s. More than a billion people live in extreme poverty (out of a world population of some 7.4 billion) and many more do not have access to basic services or social protection.

In many places in the world women's ability to fully participate in decision-making within different economic and environmental sectors is limited despite their significant role in production and consumption. In part, women's lack of empowerment stems from reduced bargaining power within communities and households.

Bargaining power is determined by a number of variables including sex, age, family structure, number of children, education, financial assets, and control or ownership of land. The specific mix of factors contributing to women's influence can vary considerably from one region to another.

Priority issues in regard to the gender-and-environment nexus

Rights to land, natural resources and biodiversity

Natural resources underpin livelihoods for the vast majority of local populations worldwide. Persistent restrictions imposed on access to natural resources by certain communities (and groups of people) are examples of the structural inequalities and discrimination that can potentially destabilize a peaceful society. This is particularly evident with respect to land tenure, but also extends to access and usage rights to renewable resources such as water, as well as equitable distribution of benefits from extractive resources including minerals, metals, timber, and oil and gas. According to the OECD's Social Institutions and Gender Index (SIGI), based on data for 160 countries, in only 37% of these countries did women and men have equal rights to own, use and control land (OECD 2014). Addressing issues of gender and other inequalities related to sustainable environmental and natural resource access, participation and decision-making can further efforts towards lasting peace and sustainable development.

Access to food, energy, water and sanitation

Unpaid care work by women and girls is of particular relevance in regard to their access to food, energy, water and sanitation. In both rural and urban areas, especially in urban slums and low-income neighbourhoods, lack of basic infrastructure and lack of energy, water and sanitation services contributes to time poverty and social and economic pressures. Women tend to be the primary energy, water and sanitation managers in most developing countries. Together with children, they bear a disproportionate burden in regard to finding and fetching water and fuel (Grassi *et al.* 2015).

The food and nutrition security of women can be disproportionately compromised because they assume great responsibility for feeding their families and communities while they often eat last and eat least. Although women produce a significant proportion of food in the developing world, mainly through smallholder farming, they remain worse fed and more undernourished than men and boys due to cultural and social norms. Providing food and nutrition security for women and girls is of foremost importance.

Well-being: climate change, sustainable consumption and production, and health

The impacts of climate change, including biodiversity loss and constraints on access to productive and natural resources, amplify existing gender inequalities and jeopardize the well-being of all. Climate change and its uncertainty put further pressure on the already fragile, under-valued and precarious gendered roles and responsibilities at community level, which shape the nature and extent of exposure, sensitivity and impacts. The gender-differentiated consequences of climate change can intensify the factors that place women who rely on agriculture and natural resources for their livelihoods at a disadvantage. As agricultural work becomes more labour-intensive or alternative sources of food and income need to be found, the burden of additional work often falls on women. Climate- and disaster-related health risks and water and fuel scarcity further add to women's unpaid care work.

Women have differentiated vulnerabilities to climate change due to gendered labour and care roles and social status, both in the case of disasters and in their everyday livelihood choices, constraints and expectations. From initial analysis focusing on women's seemingly universalized vulnerability there has been progress towards a more nuanced understanding of intersecting power relations, including clear shifts in the adoption of new roles by women and men as climate change coping strategies (Arora-Jonsson 2011, Denton 2002).

The impacts of environmental and climate challenges on family and community well-being (and on the extent of women's unpaid care work) are especially severe when health facilities and services are unavailable or unaffordable.

Women's empowerment is essential to build resilience and adapt to climate change. Gender-responsive climate change policy needs to be cognizant of and sensitive to the nuances of local and intra-household dynamics in efforts to mitigate and transform these patterns, as well as farsighted enough to support building resilience and preventing these gendered impacts from occurring.

References

Aguilar, L., Granat, M., and Owren, C. (2015). *Roots for the future: The landscape and way forward on gender and climate.* Washington, DC: IUCN and GGCA.

Arora-Jonsson, S. (2011). Virtue and vulnerability: Discourses on women, gender and climate change, *Global Environmental Change*, 21(2), 744-751.

Carson, R. (1962). *Silent Spring.* Houghton Mifflin, New York.

Denton, F. (2002). Climate change vulnerability, impacts, and adaptation: Why does gender matter?, *Gender and Development*, 10(2), 10-20.

Grassi, F., Landberg, J., Huyer, S. (2015). *Running Out of Time: The reduction of women's work burden in agricultural production.* FAO, Rome.

Harris, G.L.A. (2011). The Quest for Gender Equity, *Public Administration Review*, 71(1), 123-126.

Leach, M. (2015). *Gender Equality and Sustainable Development: Pathways to Sustainability.* Earthscan, London.

MEA (2005). *Ecosystems and Human Well-being: Synthesis.* Millennium Ecosystem Assessment (MEA), Washington, DC.

Nightingale, A. (2006). The Nature of Gender: Work, Gender, and Environment, *Environment and Planning D*: Society and Space, 24(2), 165-185.

OECD (2014). *Social Institutions and Gender Index: 2014 Synthesis Report.* The OECD Development Centre, Paris.

Razavi, S. and Qayum, S. (2015). Gender equality and sustainable development: the limits and potential of global policy reports. *In Gender Equality and Sustainable Development. Pathways to Sustainability.* Routledge/Earthscan, London and New York.

Seager, J. (2014). Background and Methodology for Gender Global Environmental Outlook. UNEP, Nairobi. [Online] Available at: http://uneplive.unep.org/community/file/download/5562/ggeo-multi-stakehoder-consultation-background-document-final

UN (2015). *Transforming Our World: The 2030 Agenda for Sustainable Development.* United Nations.

UN (2014). *World Survey on the role of women in development 2014; Gender Equality and Sustainable Development.* UN Women, New York.

UN (1995). Report of the Fourth World Conference on Women. United Nations, Beijing.

UN (1979). Convention on the Elimination of All Forms of Discrimination against Women (CEDAW). United Nations, New York.

THE GENDER AND ENVIRONMENT DIMENSION OF SUSTAINABLE DEVELOPMENT

Photo credits from left to right - first row © Matyas Rehak, UN Photo/Albert González Farran, UN Photo/Eskinder Debebe
Left to right - second row © UN Photo/Martine Perret, James Morgan / WWF-US, John Englar,
Last photo © Le Bich

CHAPTER

2

Introduction

Socially constructed gender roles often create differences in the ways women and men behave in relation to the environment, and in the ways they are enabled to act or prevented from acting as agents of environmental change. For example, simple gender-based divisions of labour can affect how women and men know and experience different elements of the environment: if only men fish in the open sea and only women fish in coastal mangroves, or if many men drive to work in a private car and most women use public transportation, they will inevitably have different sets of environmental knowledge and experience.

This different environmental positioning may mean women and men have exposures to very different environmental problems and risks, along with different perspectives on the degree of seriousness of environmental problems and on appropriate interventions, adaptations and solutions. Further, because of the social construction of gender roles, women and men may have different – usually unequal – capacities and approaches for acting as agents of environmental interpretation and change.

The GGEO methodology framework

At the heart of environmental gender analysis is curiosity about whether women and men (and girls and boys) experience the environment differently, and whether they have different needs, encounters, vulnerability and resilience. This necessitates a basic curiosity about gender equality and inequality – how inequalities are created, perpetuated, and sometimes effectively challenged and changed.

The GGEO methodological model **(Figure 1)** shows the analytical flow among Drivers-Pressures-State-Effects/Impacts-Response/Policies, which are mediated through Knowledge/Perceptions including traditional and indigenous knowledge; these then inform the Outlook on the transformative changes needed to achieve a sustainable and just future.

Figure 1: GGEO methodological model

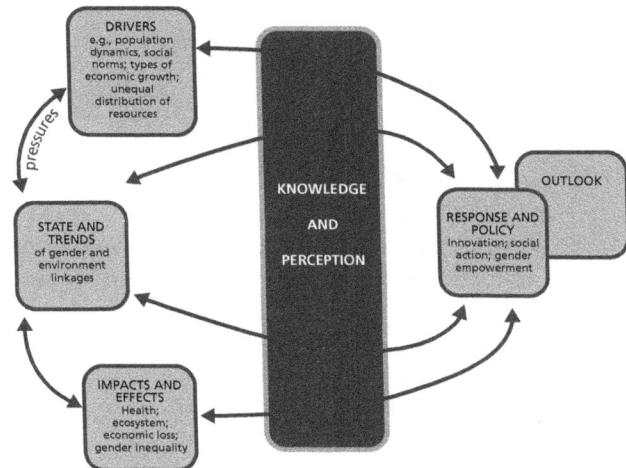

Source: Seager (2014)

To emphasize its people-oriented character and address a key challenge (the lack of gender-disaggregated information in many of the assessed areas), the GGEO methodology employs several analytical approaches:

- A human-centred analytical approach: Using this approach, environmental relationships are examined through the lens of social relationships and in the context of human economic activities, rather than the environment being defined primarily in physical terms.

- **Incorporating the social construction of knowledge:** Shifting the boundaries of environmental assessment to include qualitative and quantitative information (measurable as well as "real-world" knowledge) broadens the range of expertise on which we can draw. Among other social forces, perceptions intervene and these perceptions are inevitably gender-differentiated.

- **"Lifting the roof off the household":** Household-based, environmentally relevant decisions and behaviours are negotiated, often unequally, between women and men inside households – including on matters such as water use, the division of labour, energy-source choices and financial allocations for agricultural adaptation. Intra-household dynamics are critically important in terms of the use, conservation and consumption of resources and the ways that women and men (may) act as agents of environmental change. All environmentally consequential decisions made within households are filtered through gender norms and roles.

- **Drawing on a diverse mix of information sources:** Gender analysis recognizes the value of both quantitative and qualitative data. Quantitative information is necessary, but insufficient; it does not capture "experience" and cannot capture most aspects of "empowerment". Qualitative understanding is all the more important in view of the lack of gender-disaggregated quantitative information needed to carry out environmental assessments.

Understanding drivers, trends and interconnections

The interconnections among drivers, pressures and impacts on gender equality and environmental sustainability are complex. The relationships between gender and environment are often manifested over a long time period; in many cases, the available evidence and data do not capture these relationships fully.

The fifth *Global Environment Outlook (GEO-5)* identified population and economic development as two major drivers of environmental changes and impacts, while a range of economic activities and natural resource exploitation were also considered to put pressures on the environment (UNEP 2012). Assessing gender and environmental linkages requires a different perspective on what are the drivers and pressures of gender inequality in relation to achieving a healthy environment, as well as their contributions as agents of change. Besides demographic changes and economic development, this includes the social, political-structure and gender norms of a society.

This chapter demonstrates that gender norms and environmental changes affect each other, and their roles as drivers/pressures and effects/impacts could be interchanged. For example, environmental factors have a significant influence on the global burden of disease; it has been estimated that 23% of lost years of human health in men and more than 20% in women are attributable to the environment **(Table 1)**. Children under five are among the most affected group; it has been estimated that up to 26% of all deaths among children of this age could be prevented by an improved environment (WHO 2016). Environmental factors have a negative impact on maternal health and child mortality in many regions – often in least developing and developing countries, where they frequently contribute (among other factors) to a high fertility rates related to risks that children may not survive. This in turn may increase population pressures on the environment (Kaplan *et al.* 2015, Cleland 2013).

Similarly, armed conflicts often cause heavy and long-term damage to the environment and natural resources, which impact women and men differently in terms of migration processes, livelihood viability, resource scarcity, and the ability to carry out basic support activities such as water and fuelwood collection. In turn, inequality and unsound environmental management and environmental scarcity may lead to conflicts between different groups of users and parties (Koubi *et al.* 2014, Kennedy 2001).

Global drivers and trends establish the overarching context of life on this planet. They are ideologically and culturally rooted and include gender norms. For a more comprehensive understanding of gender equality issues, the root causes of gender inequalities need to be examined: that is, socially constructed roles and responsibilities that have resulted in centuries of domination by masculine attitudes and perceptions, definitions of problems, and the establishment of norms and values (thereby defining deviations from the norms).

Table 1. Contribution of environmental factors to human health in women and men in 2012

Disease group	Males			Females		
	Total DALYs ('000)	DALYs attributable to the environment ('000)	Percentage attributable to the environment (%)	Total DALYs ('000)	DALYs attributable to the environment ('000)	Percentage attributable to the environment
Infectious, parasitic, maternal, neonatal and nutritional causes	481 530	105 513	21.9	443 308	96 209	21.7
Noncommunicable diseases	790 449	154 587	19.6	715 852	121 637	17.0
Injuries	206 480	77 628	37.6	98 155	40 838	41.6
Total	1 478 459	337 728	22.8	1 257 315	258 684	20.6

Source: Prüss-Ustün et al. (2016)

References

Cleland, J. (2013). World population growth; past, present and future. *Environmental and Resource Economics*, 55(4), 543-554.

Kaplan, H., Hooper, P. L., Stieglitz, J., and Gurbhn, M. (2015). The Causal Relationship between Fertility and Infant Mortality. *Population in the Human Sciences: Concepts, Models, Evidence,* 361.

Kennedy, Jr., B. (2001). Environmental Scarcity and the Outbreak of Conflict, Population Reference Bureau.

Koubi, V., Spilker, G., Böhmelt, T., and Bernauer T. (2014). Do natural resources matter for interstate and intrastate armed conflict? *Journal of Peace Research* (51) 2, 227-243.

Prüss-Ustün, A., Wolf, J., Corvalán, C., Bos, R. and Neira, M. (2016). *Preventing disease through healthy environments: a global assessment of the burden of disease from environmental risks.* WHO, Geneva.

Seager, J. (2014). Background and Methodology for Gender Global Environmental Outlook. UNEP, Nairobi. [Online] Available at: http://uneplive.unep.org/community/file/download/5562/ggeo-multi-stakehoder-consultation-background-document-final

UNEP (2012). *Global environment outlook (GEO 5): Environment for the future we want.* UNEP, Nairobi.

Photo credit: © Le Bich

Key Messages

- Closing the gender gap in access to and control over resources such as land and production inputs, and in access to information and technology, would increase agricultural productivity and therefore reduce poverty and hunger.

- Subsistence farming, home food production and wild food collection (sectors heavily dominated by women) are not sufficiently valued in national and global data sets, or by research and extension services. Yet they contribute more to household food security and gender equality than does production of commodity crops, especially in times of price and market instability.

- The environmental impacts of the currently dominant high-input, large-scale model of agriculture and the failure to meet food security goals, together with the onset of the effects of climate change, have led to widespread acknowledgement that a "business-as-usual" approach to agriculture is inadequate.

- Women and men may be exposed to agricultural pesticides along different pathways. The health effects of chronic pesticide exposures on women and men vary considerably.

- The prevalence and nature of food insecurity differ across types of households and within households. Within food-scarce households, women and men typically use different strategies to cope with food insecurity.

- Agroecological approaches that consider the entire food system (including ecological, economic and social dimensions) support gender equality. Such approaches can reduce the negative environmental impacts of agriculture, promote participation and decision-making by women and men, and so contribute to both food security and food sovereignty.

2.1

Gender aspects of agricultural and food production

Globally, food production systems are under stress and are largely unsustainable in their present form. The negative environmental impacts of current agricultural practices include soil erosion and damaged soil structure; altered food web structure and function; contamination of the atmosphere, soil, groundwater and surface waters; deforestation to meet new needs for farmland; nitrogen and phosphorous losses to the ocean and inland water bodies, resulting in algal blooms and reduced fishery resources and biodiversity; greenhouse gas emissions; and unsustainable water use.

Closing the gender gap in access to and control over resources such as land and production inputs, and in access to information and technology, would increase productivity and generate a range of other social and economic benefits. Gender inequality is exacerbated in the current food production system and, at the same time, is one of the principal reasons the "agricultural sector is underperforming in many countries" (UNWomen/UNDP/UNEP/WB 2015, FAO 2011).

The prevalence and nature of food insecurity vary considerably across types of households and within households. Households headed by women, by youth (female or male) and by lesbian, gay, bisexual and transgender (LGBT) individuals are particularly affected by food insecurity (UN 2014, Boris et al. 2008, Gates 2004). These households could also be especially vulnerable to food insecurity related to natural disasters and environmental change.

Food security is about food quality and quantity. Even if the amount of food available has increased or is sufficient, lack of dietary diversity may persist along with micronutrient deficiency. For example, iron deficiency anaemia is the most frequent nutritional problem in both developing and developed countries, affecting mainly infants, children during early childhood, and pregnant women.

Access to work, land, inputs and services

Women and men tend to have different roles and responsibilities in food production. While gender-based patterns are context-specific, global trends indicate that while women play important roles in agricultural, livestock, fishery and non-timber forest product activities, they have limited access to (or control of) land, labour and finance.

Often women's contributions to agriculture are hidden or underestimated in formal statistics. Statistical systems typically focus on formal employment in agricultural sectors and on commercially related agriculture. This bias shrouds the considerable contributions to food security made by women through activities such as subsistence agriculture, collection of wild foods, and home gardening.

There are significant gender gaps in many countries regarding access and legal rights to land resources. Only one country in the world, Cape Verde, has reported that over half of agricultural holdings (50.5%) belong to women (FAO 2011). In more than half the countries in the world customary, traditional and religious practices discriminate against women even when statutory law guarantees them the same rights as men to own, control or use control land. Thus cultural norms prevent full implementation of equal-tenure legislative efforts. In 4% of countries women explicitly have no legal right to own, use and control land.

Assessments of gender equality in terms of land tenure need to include evaluations of the qualitative aspects of land ownership. Evidence from South Asia suggests that even when women own land, the plots they are allocated are often smaller and less fertile than those belonging to men (Rao 2011). Inheritance laws frequently have a direct impact on land ownership.

When land is in the hands of women, their decision-making capacity and livelihoods are improved, which is likely to have a positive impact on the health and well-being of their children (Paris et al. 2015). The consequences for women farmers of lacking security of land tenure include inefficient land use (resulting in lower yields) and reduced access to credit and to external inputs (World Bank 2011).

Access to financial services is generally a challenge for women and men who live below the poverty line. At the household level this access is exacerbated for women, who typically have less control over fixed assets that can be used as collateral. In most parts of the world female farmers and fishers generally have less access to financial services than their male counterparts. Even if women can obtain credit, traditional cultural practices often require them to relinquish control of a loan to male household members (FAO 2011). Where formal credit is not readily available, in many cases women have organized to assist each other through self-help microfinance groups.

Small-scale farming and agroecology support crop biodiversity and gender equality. Photo credit: © Kamira/ shutterstock.com

In nearly all countries for which data exist, male-headed households are more likely to use commercial fertilizers than female-headed ones. They are also much more likely to use insecticides, improved seeds and mechanized agriculture (Peterman et al. 2010). Lower use of agricultural inputs by women reflects not only credit constraints, but also lack of access to extension services and markets (Dolan 2004).

Women have a traditional role as seed collectors and savers – one that contributes to their status in many communities. The seeds saved may be traditional or improved varieties (IRDP 2014). In recent years community seed banks, which preserve local seeds, have been re-established in some areas and are frequently managed by women. This activity gives women a measure of autonomy while contributing to agrobiodiversity and climate change resilience.

Even where access to mechanized farm equipment such as tractors, tillers, mechanical weeders and seeders is relatively gender-equitable, many women are disadvantaged since such equipment is usually designed for use by men. Redesigning or making available better farming tools and equipment (and introducing or increasing the use of personal protective equipment) would improve efficiency, reduce the number of accidents in which women, men and children are harmed, and contribute to gender equity (Molineri *et al.* 2015, FAO 2011).

Globally, the use of mobile phone technology to share agricultural information (e.g. on markets, weather conditions and farming best practices) has greatly increased in the last decade or so. However, women and men do not always have equal access to information or to technology such as mobile phones, internet connections and computers **(Box 1)**.

In an analysis of 97 countries, only 5% of extension services were directed to women; further, only 15% of extension personnel were women, meaning that

in some cultures women engaged in agriculture were effectively barred from participating (FAO 2011). In Ethiopia, where traditional customs prevent male extension agents working with female farmers (World Bank and IFPRI 2010), only 12% of agricultural extension workers were female (Davis *et al.* 2010). A later study in Ethiopia (Elias *et al.* 2015) highlights the discriminatory attitudes of extension workers and underscores the close linkages between lack of credit access and level of education. Extension workers were encouraged to target resource-rich farmers, while women had poor access to resources. The authors recommend that differences between women and men in terms of productive assets be considered in the design of gender-responsive services, along with minimizing quantitative targeting of clients.

Unequal power in households

Farmers' decisions about adopting new technologies and strategies for food production are usually made within the context of households, where women and men typically have unequal power. Food production is

Box 1: Using information technology to share information useful to farmers

In several countries, such as Kenya, micro-insurance drought protection schemes are operated almost entirely through deploying mobile phone technology to provide information about growing conditions and to pay out insurance settlements (Burness Communications 2010). In 2014 the Ethiopian government piloted a programme to make agricultural extension services available via mobile phones (Ethiopia ATA 2014). Programmes for disseminating advice and good practices also exist in other countries. Nevertheless, using mobile technology may exacerbate gender differences in regard to access to information. A global survey found that women were significantly less likely than men to own mobile phones in Africa (23% less likely), the Middle East (24%) and South Asia (37%). "Household" ownership of a mobile phone did not mean women and men had equal access: 82% of married women reported that using them made their husbands suspicious and, in many cases, husbands would not allow their wives to use the phone at all (GSMA Development Fund 2012).

therefore influenced by the bargaining and decision-making power of different members of households. Strengthening women's bargaining power and their overall empowerment in households is important intrinsically, but also because gender equity in decision-making has been linked to positive outcomes with respect to food security and the well-being of children; women's disempowerment, on the other hand, is associated with poor nutritional outcomes for both women and children (Ziaei *et al.* 2014, World Bank 2010).

Key trends in food production

In many developing countries agricultural production is increasingly shifting from the household subsistence level to larger-scale production, based on community-based co-operative models or large commercial schemes. This has changed women's and men's roles in the farming system and influenced intra-household power dynamics.

Reliable data are not available – but needed – on women's involvement in subsistence farming, gathering of wild food, and home garden production, which are essential to household food security. These activities may fall outside definitions of "employment". However, indications are that women are important actors (even if not heavily dominating) in these food production systems. In the context of male migration to cities to find jobs, women who stay behind in rural areas bear an even greater food production burden.

Pesticides

There are gender differences in pesticide use, exposures, health outcomes and environmental impacts (**Figure 2**). Data on pesticide use by women and men in food production are incomplete and inconsistent. In a number of production systems in certain countries it is predominantly men who apply pesticides and are at great risk; in other countries, and on other crops, mainly women apply them. There are a number of reasons for these differences, including cultural and social norms, educational levels and awareness (Gupta *et al.* 2012).

Gender differences in the effects of chronic exposures to pesticides are related to the different physiologies of men and women. Overall, women are more biologically sensitive than men to many pesticides (Watts 2007, Hardell 2003). Moreover, in some situations of psychological distress women tend to be more vulnerable and to become victims of intentional

Figure 2: Percentage of women responding that they did not handle pesticides but washed pesticide-contaminated clothes by hand

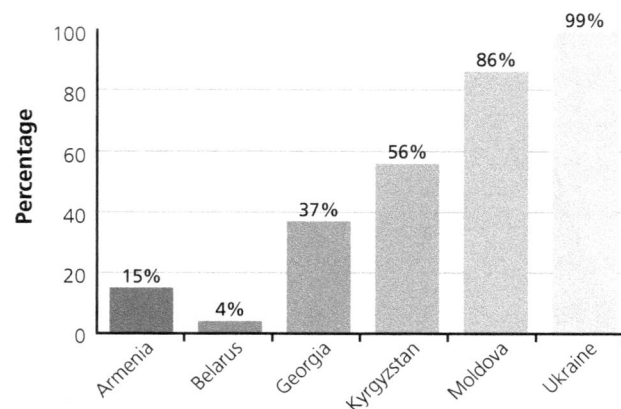

Source: FAO and PAN UK (2015)

poisoning by pesticides. There are pesticides to which men are more sensitive than women or that may have effects specific to their physiology, such as those that increase the risk of prostate cancer (Slotkin *et al.* 2008).

Gender roles in livestock tending

The gender balance of ownership, decision-making, livestock management and marketing of livestock products is highly variable. Sometimes women own (generally small) livestock, have control over the use and marketing of products such as eggs, milk and poultry meat, and make management decisions, but in other cases men exercise these functions (Staal *et al.* 2014). When livestock-based production is scaled up, control over decision-making and income often shifts to men. Male-headed households generally have larger livestock holdings (FAO 2016a, FAO 2011).

Fisheries and aquaculture

Because aquaculture is a highly nutritious source of protein and micronutrients, it is of great importance for food security. Women play a major role in aquaculture (GIZ 2013, Baluyut n.d.). In India and other countries they are involved in activities such as fingerling stocking, preparing and feeding fish, fertilizing and liming ponds, making and repairing nets, harvesting, and drying and marketing fish. Inland, men often tend to fish for cash and women for sustenance. This is also usual in many Pacific Island nations where fishing beyond the reef is often the domain of men (Dalzell *et al.* 1996) **(see also Section 2.5)**.

Agroecology and organic farming

Agroecological techniques (such as use of nitrogen-fixing green manure crops, diversified cropping, agroforestry, and beneficial insects to control pests) focus on building healthy soils, replacing external inputs with internally generated nutrients, and maintaining ecological balance.

Case studies from South Asian countries, Brazil and Malawi confirm that there are positive links between an agroecological approach, especially when supported by participatory, farmer-led group activities, and improved gender relations and social equality in farming communities (Chan and Fantle-Lepzcyk 2015, Kerr *et al.* 2013, Lopes and Jomalinis 2011).

Numerous examples support the view that women are embracing a shift to agroecology as a way not only to improve their family's food security, but also to enhance their empowerment and reduce the drudgery previously experienced in household food provision.

Gender perceptions of emerging food production issues

Animal rights in industrialized livestock production: Animal rights have long been integrated with feminist environmentalism. Since the 1970s, notably in India, Oceania, Europe and the United States, women activists have been primary drivers of animal rights movements. In a 2015 Gallup poll of attitudes to animal rights in the United States, gender-differentiated findings were significant: 42% of women said they wanted the same rights for animals as people, compared with 22% of men (Gallup 2015).

Genetically modified food: Women are generally more sceptical about the safety of GM food than men. In the United States a survey in 2015 identified significant racial and gender differences: 47% of men said eating GM food is generally safe, while only 28% of women agreed; 41% of white Americans said eating it is generally safe, while only 32% of Hispanics and 24% of African Americans agreed (Pew Research Center 2015). A 2003 global survey revealed a very large gender gap in Canada, with 73% of women saying that "genetic foods are bad" compared to 52% of men; in Japan 82% of women but only 69% of men thought genetic foods were bad (Pew Research Center 2003).

Policy and way forward

Gender inequality is at least partly a result of the dominant food production system and its drivers. Moreover, under-representation of subsistence farmers in national and global records vastly skews our understanding of women's true contributions to food production and our focus on how to improve women's empowerment in agriculture. Women's expertise, skills, knowledge, and stewardship of the genetic material in seeds are more heavily oriented towards organic, agroecological farming systems which prioritize local seed varieties, biodiversity, farm family self-provisioning, and provision to local markets where poor and hungry people can better access food (Brownhill *et al.* 2016).

References

Baluyut, E. (n.d.), *Women in Aquaculture Production in Asian Countries*. FAO, Manila.

Boris, N. W., Brown, L. A., Thurman, T. R., Rice, J. C., Snider, L. M., Ntaganira, J. and Nyirazinyoye, L. N. (2008). Depressive Symptoms In Youth Heads Of Household In Rwanda: Correlates And Implications For Intervention. *Arch Pediatr Adolesc* Med, 162, 836-43.

Brownhill, L., Njuguna E., Bothi, K.L., Pelletier, B., Lutta Muhammad, L., Hickey, G.M. (eds.). (2016). *Food Security, Gender and Resilience: Improving Smallholder and Subsistence Farming*. Earthscan/Routledge.

Burness Communications (2010). First micro-insurance plan uses mobile phones and weather stations to shield Kenya's farmers, *EurekAlert!*, American Association for the Advancement of Science, 4 March 2010.

Chan, C. and Lepczyk, J.F. (eds.) (2015). *Conservation Agriculture in Subsistence Farming: Case Studies from South Asia and Beyond*. Centre for Agriculture and Biosciences International, UK.

Dalzell, P., Adams, T.J.H. and Polunin, N.V.C. (1996). Coastal Fisheries in the Pacific Islands, *Oceanography and Marine Biology*, 34(395), 395-531.

Davis, K., Swanson, B., Amudavi, D., Mekonnen, D.A., Flohrs, A., Riese, J., C. Lamb, C. and E. Zerfu, E. (2010). In-depth Assessment of the Public Agricultural Extension System of Ethiopia and Recommendations for Improvement. *IFPRI Discussion Paper* 1041.

Dolan, C. S. (2004). "I Sell My Labour Now": Gender and Livelihood Diversification in Uganda. *Canadian Journal of Development Studies / Revue canadienne d'études du développement*, 25, 643-661.

Elias, A., Nohmi, M., Yasunobu, M. and Ishida, A. (2015). Does Gender Division of Labour Matter for the Differences in Access to Agricultural Extension Services? A Case Study in North West Ethiopia. *Journal of Agricultural Science*. 7 (1).

Ethiopia ATA (2014). *Annual Report: Transforming Agriculture in Ethiopia*. Ethiopia.

FAO (2011). *State of food and Agriculture; Women in Agriculture: Closing the Gender Gap for Development*. FAO, Rome.

FAO (2016). *Did You Know? Men and women in agriculture*. [Online] Available at: http://www.fao.org/gender/gender-home/gender-why/did-you-know/en/

FAO and PAN UK (2015). *Improved Pesticides and Chemicals Management in the Former Soviet Union*. FAO, Rome.

Gallup (2015). Animals Should be Treated as Humans: Gallup Poll, *Culture News*. [Online] Available at: http://culturecampaign.blogspot.co.ke/2015/05/animals-should-be-treated-as-humans.html.

Gates, J. G. (2014). *Food Insecurity and SNAP Participation (Food Stamps)* in LGBT Communities. Williams Institute, UCLA School of Law.

GIZ (2013). *Gender and fisheries and aquaculture,* Federal Ministry for Economic Cooperation and Development (BMZ), Bonn and Berlin.

GSMA Development Fund (2012). *Women and Mobile: A Global Opportunity A study on the mobile phone gender gap in low and middle-income countries.* GSMA, London.

Gupta, C. Gupta Vaibhav K, Nema P., Patel J. (2012). Gender Differences in Knowledge, Attitude and Practices Regarding the Pesticide Use Among Farm Workers: A Questionnaire Based Study. *Research Journal of Pharmaceutical, Biological and Chemical Sciences.* 3(3), 632-639.

Hardell, L. (2003). Environmental organochlorine exposure and the risk of breast cancer. In: Jacobs M, Dinham B (eds.). *Silent Invaders: Pesticides, Livelihoods and Women's Health.* Zed Books, London.

IRDP (2014). *Chololo Ecovillage: a Model of Good Practice in Climate Adaptation and Mitigation.* Institude for Rural Development Planning (IRDP), Tanzania.

Kerr, R.B., Shumba, L., Dakishoni, L., Lupafya, E., Berti, P.R., Classen, L., Snapp, SS. and Katundu, M. (2013). Participatory, Agroecological and Gender-Sensitive Approaches to Improved Nutrition: A Case Study in Malawi, ICN2 *Second International Conference on Nutrition: Better Nutrition, Better Lives,* FAO, Rome, and WHO, Geneva.

Lopes, A.P. and Jomalinis, E. (2011). Agroecology: *Exploring Opportunities for Women's Empowerment Based on experiences from Brazil,* ActionAid Brazil.

Molineri, A.I., Signorini-Porchietto, M.L. and Tarabla, H.D. (2015). Hazards for Women and Children in Rural Settings, *Revista de Salud Publica* (Bogota), 17(1), 22-32.

Paris, T., Pede, V., Luis, J., Sharma, R.C., Singh, A., Stipular, J. and Villanueva, D. (2015). Understanding Men's and Women's Access to and Control of Assets and the Implications for Agricultural Development Projects. A Case study in rice-farming households in Eastern Uttar Pradesh, India. Discussion Papers. International Food Policy Research Institute (IFPRI), 1437.

Peterman, A., J. Behrman, and A. Quisumbing (2010). A Review of Empirical Evidence on Gender Differences in Nonland Agricultural Inputs, Technology, and Services in Developing Countries. IFPRI Discussion Paper 00975. International Food Policy Research Institute, Washington, DC.

Pew Global Attitudes (2003). Broad opposition to genetically modified food, [Online] Available at: http://www.pewglobal. org/2003/06/20/broad-opposition-to-genetically-modified-foods/#about-this-survey

Pew Research Centre (2015). Public and Scientists Views on Science and Society. [Online] Available at: http://www.pewinternet. org/2015/01/29/public-and-scientists-views-on-science-and-society/.

Rao, N. (2011). Women's access to land: An Asian perspective. In *Expert paper prepared for the UN Group Meeting 'Enabling Rural Women's Economic Empowerment: Institutions, Opportunities and Participation'.* Accra, 20-23.

Slotkin, T. A., Bodwell, B. E., Levin, E. D. and Seidler, F. J. (2008). Neonatal exposure to low doses of diazinon: long-term effects on neural cell development and acetylcholine systems. *Environmental Health Perspect,* 116, 340-8.

Staal, S., MacMillan, S., Escarcha, J. and Grace, D. (2014). Livestock farming boosts local economies in developing countries. In: Griffiths, J. (ed). *Deep Roots.* FAO, Rome.

UN (2014). *World survey on the role of women in development: Gender Equality and Sustainable Development.* UN Women, New York.

UN Women/UNDP/UNEP/World Bank (2015). *The Cost of the Gender Gap in Agricultural Productivity in Malawi, Tanzania, and Uganda.*

Watts, M.A. (2007). Pesticides and Breast Cancer: *A Wake Up Call.* Pesticide Action Network, Asia and the Pacific, Penang.

World Bank (2010). *Understanding the Dynamics of Gender and Nutrition in Bangladesh: Implications for Policy and Programming.* World Bank, Washington, DC.

World Bank (2011). *World Development Report 2011: Conflict Security and Development.* World Bank, Washington, DC.

World Bank and IFPRI (2010). Gender and Governance in rural services: Insights from India, Ghana, and Ethiopia. *ARD Notes* (53), Washington DC.

Ziaei, S., Naved, R.T. And Ekstrom, E.C. (2014). Women's exposure to intimate partner violence and child malnutrition: findings from demographic and health surveys in Bangladesh. *Maternal and Child Nutrition,* 10(3):347-359.

Key Messages

- Water use, supply and access are associated primarily with the hydrological cycle. Understanding that there is also a "hydro-social cycle" draws attention to gender differences. Every stage in the hydro-social cycle entails different demands, risks and benefits for women and men.

- It is largely women's responsibility everywhere to manage household needs for water. This responsibility becomes even greater in the face of pervasive water quality problems in both developed and developing countries, which are likely to become worse with climate disruption.

- Within households, women and men typically express different views on water priorities and the solutions to water deficits.

- Women and girls remain the primary water collectors in households where piped water is not available, which can place them at risk of violence and sexual assault.

- The gendered profile of water collection varies with access to mechanization: men assume water collection responsibilities mostly when mechanized transport is available.

- The health effects of polluted or poor quality water are gendered. More males than females suffer and die from diarrhoea in every region except Southeast Asia.

- Public toilet provision for women almost everywhere in the world lags far behind that for men. Absence or inadequate provision of public toilets for women reflects and reinforces the exclusion of women from public power and public space more generally.

- Gender inequity in access to toilets has stimulated robust activist movements that are shifting toilet and menstrual hygiene management needs from being considered a "private" concern to a "public" one.

- Women are poorly represented in staffing and formal employment in the water and sanitation sectors.

2.2

Recognizing the gendered dimensions of water, sanitation and hygiene

The hydro-social cycle

Access to and control over water, and water management and use, are shaped as much by social factors (including gendered power relations) as by physical ones. Every stage in the hydro-social cycle involves different demands, risks and benefits for women and men (Joshi 2015, Zwarteveen et al. 2012, Seager et al.2009, Sultana 2007, UN-Water 2006).

Policy and legislation

The need for gender equality in provision of clean water and sanitation has been recognized in numerous national policies and multilateral agreements since the late 1970s. Gender analysis is still limited overall and has been introduced unevenly. A 2012 UN-Water report on national water and sanitation policies revealed that fewer than 40% of the 64 responding countries included specific equity provisions in national strategy or funding decisions that addressed women's rights to water, and fewer than 20% had applied or implemented those addressing women's right to sanitation (WHO and UN-Water 2012). Only a few countries had national policies that included specific provisions to meet women's needs, including menstrual hygiene management **(Figure 3)**.

Formal employment and decision-making

Women are poorly represented in staffing and formal employment in the water and sanitation sectors. Half the governments that responded to the 2011 Global

Figure 3: GLAAS survey of governments: Do national sanitation and drinking-water policies/strategies include specific provisions for women, including menstrual hygiene management needs?

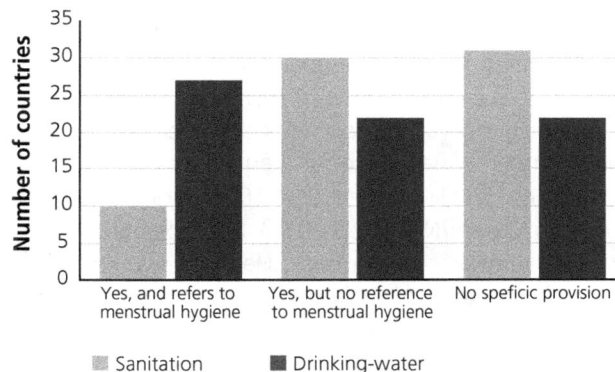

Source: WHO and UN-Water (2012)

Analysis and Assessment of Sanitation and Drinking-Water (GLAAS) survey reported that women made up less than 10% of the professional and managerial staff in these sectors (WHO and UN-Water 2012). Even when women are participants in formal decision-making processes, their interests are rarely taken into account due to gender-related inequalities and restrictive definitions of appropriate female behaviour.

Water use, access, quality, production and distribution

Water poverty, time poverty, access and use

Women and men everywhere are affected by water availability, access and quality, but in different ways due to prevailing gender roles and norms. In settings where water must be collected from a source outside the home, women and girls have the main responsibility for collecting it.

Water-related chores often keep girls from going to school (UNICEF 2012, Haggart and McGuire n.d.). In addition, time spent collecting water diminishes women's overall ability to control their own time and participate in other pursuits, whether these are waged work, recreation, cultural activities or political involvement. It also represents a tremendous economic loss: in India, for example, it has been estimated that women spend 150 million work days per year fetching and carrying water, the equivalent of a national loss of income of 10 billion rupees (US$160 million) (WaterAid/Unilever/Oxfam/NextDrop 2015); a Sub-Saharan survey in 25 countries reveals that collectively women spent a combined total of at least 16 million hours per day collecting drinking water, men 6 million and children 4 million (UNICEF and WHO 2012).

In many cases the water collection burden could be alleviated through changes in transport. The gendered profile of water collection varies with access to mechanization. Men and boys are much more likely to collect water when they can use mechanized transport such as bikes, scooters and trucks. A survey of water collection in Mongolia showed that in Ulaanbaatar men made up the majority of water collectors across all forms of water collection, but were particularly prominent in water collection by vehicle and by animal (Hawkins and Seager 2010). In rural Kenya 87% of women who collected water reportedly did so without mechanical assistance, compared with 42% of men (WHO 2011).

Evidence to date concerning water supply privatization suggests that it often leads to increased water use efficiency, but also to increased pressure on the poorest, who may be almost entirely unable to pay.

Water, health and security

Water collection can be dangerous, especially for women. Walking to remote locations to collect water for drinking, cooking and clothes washing or to use water, sanitation and hygiene (WASH) facilities, particularly after dark, puts women and girls at risk of harassment, sexual assault and rape (Anand 2014, Amnesty International 2010).

Women and girls in conflict-affected settings routinely experience physical insecurity, including sexual violence, when performing daily tasks linked to use of natural resources such as fuel, wood and water (UNEP/UN Women/UNPSO/UNDP 2013). It is also not uncommon in conflict and post-conflict situations for men and boys to be vulnerable to abduction, murder or rape when they visit water points outside camp boundaries (House et al. 2014).

Water shortages due to long-term climate change, short-term weather fluctuations, disasters and conflict have gendered dimensions. Individuals' capacities to cope with physical and food insecurity, displacement, loss of livelihood assets, social exclusion and other impacts are strongly influenced by gendered roles and responsibilities.

Head-loading, a common way to carry water in several parts of the world, is gendered. Almost no men carry water in this way. A study in South Africa found that for women who head-carried, catastrophic spinal injury and knee injuries were not uncommon; there were also frequent accidents as women and girls carried water burdens that could easily weigh 40% of their own body weight along uneven pathways and roads (Geere et al. 2010).

It has been estimated that improving water, sanitation, hygiene and water resource management globally could prevent around 10% of the global disease burden and more than 6% of all deaths (Prüss-Üstün et al. 2008). Of the almost 2 million total global deaths in 2004 attributed to unsafe WASH, 48% were female and 52% male (UN DESA 2012). The gender profile for deaths from diarrhoea due to poor water and sanitation is consistent across most regions: more males suffer and die from diarrhoea everywhere except Southeast Asia, where the share of female deaths and illness is notable and produces a global tilt towards higher female deaths and DALYs overall (Prüss-Üstün et al. 2014) **(Table 2)**.

Sanitation and wastewater

Sanitation access and use

In 2015 an estimated 2.4 billion people did not have access to improved sanitation (UNICEF and WHO 2015). The number of people without access to safe sanitation is under-recorded, but is likely to be several orders of magnitude higher.

Monitoring gender inequalities in access to improved sanitation is challenging. While some cross-sectional surveys (e.g. on health) may assess disparities in access to sanitation between female- and male-headed households, they seldom provide data at the individual level, where access to sanitation really counts. To better understand the gendered nature of access to improved sanitation, new indicators are required that provide detailed gender-disaggregated data at the intra-household level.

The great majority of rural households rely on pit latrines outside their dwellings. Individuals resort to open defecation if there is no space for latrines. In urban slums and informal settlements there is usually no room to build latrines, or there are no tenure or property rights that would make this possible. Open defecation is generally a greater health and safety risk for women and girls, especially during menstruation; it

Table 2: Deaths and disability-adjusted life years (DALYs) from diarrhoea due to poor water and sanitation

Region	Deaths (male)	Deaths (female)	DALYs (male)	DALYs (female)
Africa	186 130	181 476	14 408 971	13 764 653
Americas (low and middle income)	6 021	5 525	498 565	443 354
Eastern Mediterranean (low and middle income)	41 227	39 838	3 337 950	3 154 444
Europe (low and middle income)	1 890	1 675	191 048	175 136
Southeast Asia	150 179	213 725	8 101 272	10 786 489
Western Pacific region (low and middle income)	7 626	6 536	869 126	740 089
Total	393 073	448 775	27 406 932	29 064 165

Source: Prüss-Üstün et al. (2014)

may also put them in a position of contravening socially constructed notions of appropriate feminine behaviour (Wendland *et al.* 2012). WaterAid, an NGO, estimates that one in three women worldwide lacks access to safe toilets, risking not only shame and disease but also sexual assaults and attacks (WaterAid 2012).

Lack of suitable sanitation provision in schools can prevent girls receiving an education. Schools without toilets, or with shared toilets, pose health and safety risks. They also represent a significant cultural barrier that can keep girls away from such schools (Roma and Pugh 2012).

On a larger scale, toilet provision reflects broad equality struggles. The absence of public toilets for women is associated with their exclusion from public power and from public spaces more generally (Plaskow 2008). In some parts of the world transgender rights movements, and actions by other citizens who are sensitive to the needs of transgender people, are calling attention to the need for appropriate transgender toilet facilities (Johnston 2016).

Menstrual hygiene management and sanitation facilities

Menstrual hygiene management (MHM) is essential to ensure gender equality. Without appropriate provisions, women cannot fully participate in all aspects of society and economy. The absence of adequate sanitation facilities for menstrual hygiene has direct impacts on women's rights to education, to work and to health (George 2013). Very few countries have national targets for menstrual hygiene promotion programmes, and only about 2% of total WASH expenditure is used for menstrual hygiene promotion (WHO and UN-Water 2012). A consequence (as well as a cause) of official inattention to MHM is a lack of robust gender-segregated data on sanitation policies and technologies.

The greatest progress in regard to MHM has occurred as a result of community activism, which is breaking taboos and gaining popular and official attention. In 2015 a "Breaking the Silence" campaign in South Asia won a national media awareness award (Chanam 2015); in 2013, WASH United, an NGO, initiated a global Menstrual Hygiene Day on 28 May (Keiser 2013).

Sustainable sanitation and wastewater management

Provision and management of sustainable sanitation and wastewater management are of basic importance not only for environmental sustainability, but also for gender equality. Long experience has shown that sustainability in sanitation and wastewater management requires more than toilets and infrastructure. It also requires social change in which women play a key role, together with reliable long-term financing, new or adapted institutional structures, monitoring and testing, and co-ordination and joint planning across government sectors including health, water, energy, agriculture and environment.

There are recent trends towards the development of environmentally sustainable sanitation systems, which are increasingly under consideration as feasible and affordable alternatives for rural municipalities, low-income small communities, or groups of households (Wendland and Albold 2010). These systems range from natural approaches such as use of ponds and constructed wetlands (which are low-tech and low-maintenance) as filters and for cleaning wastewater, to high-tech vacuum biogas installations.

References

Amnesty International (2010). *Insecurity and Indignity: Women's experiences in the slums of Nairobi, Kenya.* Amnesty International, UK.

Anand, A. (2014). Lack of toilets puts India's health and rural women's safety at risk, *Guardian*. [Online] Available at: http://www.theguardian.com/global-development/2014/aug/28/toilets-india-health-rural-women-safety.

Chanam, Urmila. (2015). Breaking the Silence Campaign: From Shame to Pride in Pakistan. [Online] Available at: https://www.worldpulse.com/en/community/users/urmila-chanam/posts/36420.

Geere, J.A., Hunter, P.R. and Jagals, P. (2010). Domestic water carrying and its implications for health: a review and mixed methods pilot study in Limpopo Province, South Africa, *Environ Health*, 9:52, 1-13.

George, R. (2013). Celebrating Womanhood: How Better Menstrual Hygiene Management is the Path to Better Health, Dignity and Business, *International Women's Day Event, March 2013*. Geneva.

Haggart, K. and McGuire, C. *Struggling for safe access to water and sanitation.* [Online] Available at: http://www.idrc.ca/EN/Resources/Publications/Pages/ArticleDetails.aspx?PublicationID=1168

Hawkins, R. and J.Seager (2012). Gender and Water in Mongolia. Professional Geographer, Vol 62 #1, February

House, S., Ferron, S., Sommer, M. and Cavill, S. (2014). V*iolence, gender and WASH: a practitioners toolkit. Making water, sanitation and hygiene safer through improved programming.* WaterAid/SHARE, London.

Johnston, L. (2016). 'You can't use that bathroom': Transgendering public toilets. *New Zealand Geographical Society Conference (NZGS): Geographical Interactions.*

Joshi, D. (2015). Like water for justice, *Geoforum*, 61, 111-121.

Keiser, D. (2013). How a Menstruation-themed Social Media Campaign Spurred a Movement for a Global Awareness Day. Period. *Bill and Melinda Gates Foundation* [Online] Aavailable at: http://www.impatientoptimists.org/Posts/2013/07/How-a-Menstruationthemed-Social-Media-Campaign-Spurred-a-Movement-for-a-Global-Awareness-Day-Period#.VzuahWY7Q-8.

Plaskow, J. (2008). Embodiment, Elimination, and the Role of Toilets in Struggles for Social Justice, *CrossCurrents*, 58(1), 51-64.

Prüss-Üstün A., Bos, R., Gore, F. and Bartram, J. (2008). *Safer water, better health: costs, benefits and sustainability of interventions to protect and promote health.*World Health Organization, Geneva.

Prüss-Üstün A., Bartram, J., Clasen, T., Colford, J.M., Jr., Cumming, O., Curtis, V., Bonjour, S., Dangour, A.D., De France, J., Fewtrell, L. *et al.* (2014). Burden of disease from inadequate water, sanitation and hygiene in low- and middle-income settings: a retrospective

analysis of data from 145 countries, *Trop Med Int Health*, 19(8), 894-905.

Roma, E and I. Pugh. (2012). *Toilets for Health.* London School of Hygiene and Tropical Medicine, in collaboration with Domestos.

Seager, J., Robinson, K., van der Schaaf, C., Gabizon, S. (2009). *Gender-Disaggregated Data on Water and Sanitation.* NY: UN DESA.

Sultana, F. (2007). Water, Water Everywhere, But Not a Drop to Drink: Pani Politics (Water Politics) in Rural Bangladesh, *International Feminist Journal of Politics*, 9(4), 494-502.

UN DESA (2010). *The world's women 2010: Trends and statistics.* United Nations, New York.

UN Water (2006). Gender, Water and Saniatation: A Policy Brief. [Online] Available at: http://www.unwater.org/downloads/unwpolbrief230606.pdf.

UNEP, UN Women, UNPSO and UNDP (2013). Women and Natural Resources: *Unlocking the Peacebuilding Potential.* D.J. and S. Halle (Eds). UNEP, Nairobi, UN Women, PBSO and UNDP, New York.

UNICEF (2012). *Raising even more clean hands: Advancing health, learning and equity through WASH in schools.* UNICEF.

UNICEF and WHO (2012). *Progress on Drinking Water and Sanitation: 2012* Update and MDG assessment.

UNICEF and WHO (2015). *Progress on Sanitation and Drinking Water: 2015* Update and MDG assessment.

WaterAid, Unilever, Oxfam and NextDrop (2015). *Water for Women: Every Woman Counts. Every Second Counts.*

WaterAid (2012). Briefing note: 1 in 3 women lack access to safe toilets.

Wendland, C., Dankelman, I., Ruben, C., Kunze, I., Sommer, M. and Mbalo, D. (2012). Integrating a gender perspective in sustainable sanitation - *Factsheet of Working Group 7b.* Sustainable Sanitation Alliance (SuSanA).

Wendland, C. and Albold, A. (2010). Constructed Wetlands; Sustainable Wastewater Treatment for Rural and Peri-Urban communities in Bulgaria. WECF.

WHO (2011). *Valuing Water, Valuing Livelihoods. Guidance on social cost-benefit analysis of drinking-water interventions, with special reference to small community water supplies.* WHO, Geneva.

WHO and UN Water (2012). *GLAAS 2012 Report: UN-water global analysis and assessment of sanitation and drinking-water (GLAAS): the challenge of extending and sustaining services.* UN Water and WHO, Geneva.

Zwarteveen, M., S. Ahmed and Suman, R.G. (2012). *Diverting the flow: Gender equity and water in South Asia.* Zubaan Books, New Delhi.

Key Messages

- Using renewable and sustainable energy can catalyze gender equality, but this type of energy is not inevitably socially and environmentally friendly. Without the use of a social justice lens for energy planning, large-scale renewable energy projects can be environmentally damaging and may do little to enhance gender equality.

- Decision-making in the formal energy sectors is heavily gender-skewed, as are staffing and formal employment. Decision-making in the energy sector often excludes women, and policies are mostly gender-unaware.

- There are significant gender differences in perceptions of current energy options, and of the risks and choices relating to various energy technologies.

- Insecure land ownership and energy-related land grabbing have different gendered impacts.

- At the community and grassroots levels, women and men are not waiting for top-down energy transformation. In many cases they are creating their own pathways to clean energy technology that level the playing field in regard to economic and social opportunity.

- In developing countries the time spent, predominantly by women, in collecting biomass-based energy supplies is responsible for tremendous time poverty and foregone opportunities.

- In both developed and developing countries energy poverty is a large and often invisible problem, and one which is gendered.

- Pervasive lack of gender-differentiated data has implications for the assessment of technology needs with respect to technical training and capacity building activities. It has the potential to reduce development initiatives directed at gender and energy since the deep inequalities in the energy sector cannot easily be quantified.

- A priority for all energy plans should be to make safe and sustainable household energy available to the 3 billion people who currently do not have it. Enabling the creation of local renewable energy user groups and co-operatives, and empowering women to fully participate at all levels of decision-making, is essential for sustainable energy.

2.3

Energy divides: global, social and gendered

Energy production and consumption are key drivers of livelihoods, economies and environmental conditions. Since 1990 overall global energy use has increased by more than 50%; in 2015 ten countries consumed about two-thirds of the world's energy (Enerdata 2015, GCEC 2014). Average per capita energy consumption is high in developed countries and lowest in the least developed ones (World Bank 2015). Lack of energy is a barrier to development.

Socially constructed gender roles, identities and underlying power dynamics affect whether and how women and men access and use energy and participate in decisions and investments. Surveys have repeatedly shown that women and men express different energy needs and priorities and perceive different risks in regard to energy choices.

In the least developed countries, women who play traditional roles as primary household managers suffer most from lack of access to adequate energy. Decentralized renewable and efficient energy-related technologies could make a major economic and social difference for many rural women if they resulted in increased income. However, acquiring energy equipment is expensive. The lending expectations of banks and credit institutions often disadvantage women and, in many countries, women still face legal restrictions that keep them from accessing credit in their own name or without the consent of their husbands.

Millions of people in North America, Eastern Europe, Central Asia and other parts of the developed world suffer from energy poverty (CAFOD 2015). Energy poverty in developed countries affects elderly women and female single parents in particular (Pye and Dobbin 2015). The number of households whose energy supply is temporarily interrupted because of unpaid bills is increasing in many European countries, and recent research shows the number of countries with "vulnerable consumers" is increasing (Pye and Dobbin 2015).

Gender aspects of centralized energy planning and policy

Gender in energy planning

Gender aspects in the planning and policy cycles and sectors have little visibility in formal and centralized policy frameworks. Globally gender is scarcely mainstreamed in energy policies, even in the case of the newest energy sectors. As of early 2015, 145 countries had enacted policies to regulate and promote renewables in the power generation, heating and cooling, and transport sectors, the majority of which are not gender-sensitive (REN21 2015).

Some shifts are evident. Uganda's Renewable Energy Policy has special gender strategies, including promotion of microfinance, to ensure that women can benefit from renewable energy technologies in their household tasks. India's national biofuels programme specifically refers to the role of women in cultivating biodiesel crops. The Kenyan government has made considerable progress on recognizing the gender-and-environment nexus. At COP21, where 140 countries presented their plans for emission reductions (Intended Nationally Determined Contributions or INDCs), some 50 countries submitted

INDCs that referred to gender as important in combatting climate change (Rojas *et al.* 2015).

Energy policies typically focus on issues of investment, tariffs, pricing, access, availability, infrastructure development, participation and environment (Woroniuk and Schalkwyk 1998). All these issues are intrinsically linked to gender roles and responsibilities, although energy policy is often erroneously considered gender-neutral.

In the absence of gender-disaggregated data on energy use, needs and access, macro-level energy policies that focus on topics such as investment, imports and pricing will continue to be gender-blind. Throughout the energy sector, in all its diversity, gender-disaggregated data are mostly missing (and are needed) on energy-related needs, preferences, income and expenditures, decision-making, benefits and impacts, staffing, employment, and access to credit and information (Cecelski 2002).

Gendered leadership and participation in formal planning and policy

Women are under-represented in national government positions of importance to the energy sector, with only 7% female ministers in the fields of environment, natural resources and energy and 3% in science and technology (UNIDO and UN Women 2013). In the European Union in 2011 high-level positions in national ministries covering environmental affairs were occupied by men in 66.1% of cases compared with 33.9% by women (EIGE 2012). In international decision-making processes concerned with responding to climate change, which will require transforming the energy sector, most negotiators are men. Consequently, the fora in which energy issues are identified and potential solutions proposed are likely to have an inadvertent male bias (UNIDO and UN Women 2013). In addition to the leadership gap, the share of women in the workforce in the energy sector is generally quite low.

Energy production, supply and consumption

Energy production at zero monetary cost: on the shoulders of women

Almost 3 billion people, most of whom live in Asia and Sub-Saharan Africa, rely on open fires and traditional biomass such as wood, dung and crop waste for cooking and heating (WHO 2015, IEA 2014). Reflecting gendered social norms, women and children perform a large share of the unpaid work required to collect biomass fuels, with differences according to regions and types of fuel. Depending on region, season and availability, average biomass collection time in Africa is estimated at four to ten hours per week (World LP Gas Association 2014, Matinga 2010).

While biomass energy sources are collected without direct financial outlays ("at no cost"), the indirect economic costs are enormous in terms of missed opportunities for employment, education and self-improvement, all of which are essential to improve community livelihoods. A World Bank report argues that much of this unpaid work could be reduced or eliminated by, among other interventions, improving infrastructure for energy and other services. These interventions would result in a higher gross domestic product (GDP), lead to women's financial independence, and possibly have a ripple effect on intergenerational benefits, as research in 24 countries has shown that daughters of mothers who work for pay are more likely to be employed themselves and to have supervisory roles (World Bank 2015).

Social costs and benefits of expanding the electricity grid

Expanding the grid and extending the reach of electricity is a critical goal for gender empowerment, social equity and eliminating poverty. In low- and middle-income countries energy expansion is proceeding rapidly, often by means of large-scale energy projects. Large-scale energy projects (including for renewable energy such as hydropower) not uncommonly result in displacement of local communities. Although there has been progress in recent years on laws recognizing women's land ownership, women are still particularly disadvantaged by displacement (Davis and Fisk 2014). Globally less than 20% of land titles are registered in women's names (less than 10% in most parts of Africa) and if compensation is provided for dislocation of communities due to large-scale energy projects, women are compensated at lower levels – if at all – because of their invisibility in land titling and claims processes. Communal land use is often not recognized (Skinner 2016).

Women may have greater difficulty recovering from dislocations. If compensation by governments or companies for large-scale project displacement includes compensation for lost employment, women who work in the informal sector and do not have an official employment record will have no basis for a formal claim. Construction of large energy installations often provides employment to local people. Although there has been little research on this topic, given patterns in other labour sectors – in industrialized countries 65-90% of all part-time workers are women (ILO and EU 2011, ILO 1995) – if women are hired they are likely to make up a greater share of the informal and part-time workers that such projects require.

Women's entrepreneurship in small-scale energy service delivery

In both developed and developing countries women's best chance of becoming involved in sustainable energy provision is at the community level. Many women-led sustainable energy initiatives in the community energy sector have been successful. Business models for small-scale energy production range from consignment arrangements, to linking of entrepreneurs to micro-financing institutions (possibly through the use of loan guarantee funds, which lowers the risk for financing institutions), to women individually or in groups taking on the manufacture or assembly of devices (sometimes as part of family businesses), to women's networks raising awareness of, for example, policy, options, pricing and safety **(Box 2)**.

Gender differences in energy consumption

In the area of energy consumption it is crucial to "lift the roof off the household" to analyze access, use and needs not only by "household" but by gender. Analysis of gender differences in energy consumption is an emerging area of research that is not yet well developed.

Box 2: Entrepreneurial opportunities for women in renewables

wPower: The United States Department of State launched the Partnership on Women's Entrepreneurship in Renewables (wPOWER) in January 2013. wPOWER aims to empower more than 8000 women clean energy entrepreneurs across East Africa, Nigeria and India, who will deliver clean energy access to more than 3.5 million people over the next three years.

A wPower partner in India, Swayam Shikshan Prayog, has trained more than 1000 women to be entrepreneurs selling clean energy and renewable household technologies (SSP 2016). Another wPower partner, Solar Sister, established in 2010, has worked with more than 1200 women entrepreneurs in Uganda, Nigeria and the United Republic of Tanzania. Solar Sister equips women to build their own technology-driven businesses by providing a holistic package of inputs including business and technical training, access to products and service, marketing support and ongoing coaching. A study conducted by the International Center for Research on Women (ICRW) in 2012 showed that the Solar Sister Entrepreneurs earn an average of US$48 a month, a significant amount compared to average incomes in the region. There are also indirect economic benefits. As users of solar lanterns, the women can save about 30% of fuel expenses on kerosene (paraffin); less time spent collecting fuelwood means more time for other pursuits (Gill *et al.* 2012).

Concerning energy use in the transport sector, for example, gender differences seem fairly consistent across countries. Since transport is a great and growing climate polluter (23% of overall CO_2 emissions globally, with a high growth rate) (Kahn *et al.* 2007), it is useful to look at these differences. A recent study in Spain reflects almost universal findings that women make greater use of more sustainable (walking and public) transport than men in both urban and rural areas: in urban municipalities 48.3% of women's trips were made by walking and 25.4% by public transport, compared to 34% and 18.6%, respectively, of men's trips; in rural areas fewer women used private transport than men: 62.1% and 74.7%, respectively. The study concluded that the modal asymmetry between women and men is structural and related to masculinity expressed in relation to private transport and the "performance" of gender in everyday life (Miralles-Guasch *et al.* 2015).

Energy and health

Biomass health impacts

Cooking and heating with solid fuels (wood, charcoal, crop waste, dung and coal) produces high levels of indoor air pollution that can lead to a wide range of child and adult diseases, including acute and chronic respiratory conditions (e.g. pneumonia, chronic obstructive pulmonary disease), lung cancer, ischemic heart disease, stroke and cataracts (WHO 2015). Exposure to household air pollution (HAP) from biomass burning kills over 4 million people per year. Millions more suffer from cancer, pneumonia, heart and lung disease, blindness and burns; smoke from cooking fires is associated with cataracts, the leading cause of blindness in the world, and other health problems (Prüss-Ustün *et al.* 2016, GACC 2013, WHO n.d.). The premature deaths of more than 2 million women and children annually due to household air pollution are directly related to use of solid fuels for cooking and heating. In the premature deaths of almost 2 million men associated with HAP other factors such as smoking also play an important role (Prüss-Ustün *et al.* 2016, WHO 2014). The first step towards cleaner and safer use of fuels is to move away from open fires to better cooking technologies including improved cookstoves.

The physical burden of collecting, transporting and processing solid fuels also creates significant health problems. For example, the effect of head-loads on women's bodies is very damaging (Geere *et al.* 2010, Matinga 2010) **(Box 3)**.

> **Box 3: Average weight of fuelwood head-loads that women carry**
>
> Malawi, Tanzania and Botswana: 27-31 kg
> Ethiopia: 36 kg
> Congo: 25-50 kg
> South Africa: 24 and 38 kg in different regions
>
> *Source: Matinga (2010)*

Pollution from conventional energy production

Airborne pollution has become an especially pressing issue in countries where industrial growth has been rapid but environmental controls are weak. Technologies currently in use in many rapidly industrializing countries produce high emissions of air pollutants. Recent research confirms that large numbers of premature deaths are due to air pollution linked to small particles and mercury in emissions from coal-fired power plants. Emissions from these plants are linked to dozens of diseases including cancer and asthma (WHO 2013). There is preliminary evidence that women, children and older adults are particularly vulnerable to PM_{10} and to $PM_{2.5}$ (particulate matter 10 and 2.5 micrometres or less in diameter) (Villeneuve *et al.* 2015, Sacks *et al.* 2011).

Gender, energy transitions, and renewables

Renewable energy and energy efficiency can significantly reduce air pollution resulting from energy use and improve public health. Replacing polluting fossil fuels with renewable energy sources can reduce premature mortality and the number of lost workdays, thereby lowering overall healthcare costs (Machol and Rizk 2013). The potential health benefits include reduced symptoms of respiratory and cardiovascular conditions, rheumatism, arthritis and allergies, as well as fewer injuries (OECD and IEA 2014). Renewables and energy efficiency can be game changers for energy – and gender – poverty.

Renewable energy is not inherently socially and environmentally benign. Large-scale energy projects (including for renewables such as hydropower) not uncommonly result in displacement of local communities. Although there has been progress in recent years on laws increasing women's land ownership, women are still particularly disadvantaged by displacement (Davis and Fisk 2014). Biofuel production can diminish food security through land use change or rising food prices. Active evaluation and monitoring for gender, social, and environmental impacts are just as important for sustainable and gender-just renewable energy as in the case of conventional energy.

Gender gaps and inequalities in the renewable energy sector, in terms of employment and education, are in many instances comparable to those in the conventional energy sector. Nevertheless, positive examples point towards the possibilities of a gender-balanced and gender-responsive renewable energy sector.

Technologies to enable a transition to better household energy solutions have often proved unsatisfactory when the specific needs of women (as the main users, in their traditional roles) were not taken into account. For example, solar cookers, which work only in the daytime, do not allow flexibility in meal preparation times. In a survey of 42 renewable energy companies in Asia, Africa and Latin America, a number of entrepreneurs indicated they felt that involving women in the design of equipment (e.g. improved cookstoves) for use in the home was important to the ultimate success of their products (REN21 2015). Involving women and men in developing technologies to ensure a transition to safe and more sustainable energy is crucial for success.

Gendered perceptions of energy technology choices

A wide range of research shows that women are less positive about emerging and possibly risky technologies for energy production (Boudet et al. 2014).

Nuclear energy: In a European Union survey more women than men said nuclear energy should constitute a lower share of overall energy production (EC 2007). In the United Kingdom the level of support for building new nuclear power stations shows a 40% discrepancy, with considerably more men wanting to see new power plants built (Populus 2011). In a study in the United States 72%

of men favoured nuclear power as a source of electricity while only 42% of women did so; a correspondingly large gender gap existed in views about the safety of nuclear power plants (Newport 2012). In Australia a 2015 survey found that 19% of men favoured nuclear power as one of three energy preferences, compared with 8% of women (Hasham 2015).

Hydraulic fracturing ("fracking"): Similar results have been found in attitudes to fracking to extract natural gas trapped in shale formations. Studies, mainly in the United States, showed that women and men who associated the process with environmental threats were most likely to oppose fracking (Boudet et al. 2014, Brasier et al. 2013). A 2013 survey on knowledge about (and support for) fracking identified a significant gender gap **(Figure 4)**.

Renewables: Some evidence suggests that women also support a transition to renewable energy more strongly than men. In Australia wind power was preferred by more women (76%) than men (60%); in the same survey women were also slightly more likely to favour solar power (Hasham 2015).

The way forward

Renewable energies are projected to grow significantly in the near future. Moderate outlooks project a renewable energy share of 30-45% by 2050 (REN21 2013). Energy efficiency is predicted to make even greater advances. Governments will need effective policies to support this major transformation of energy markets and infrastructure. If the following conditions are met, renewable energy development can be a very powerful catalyst for gender equality:

Figure 4: Perceptions of and support for fracking in the United States

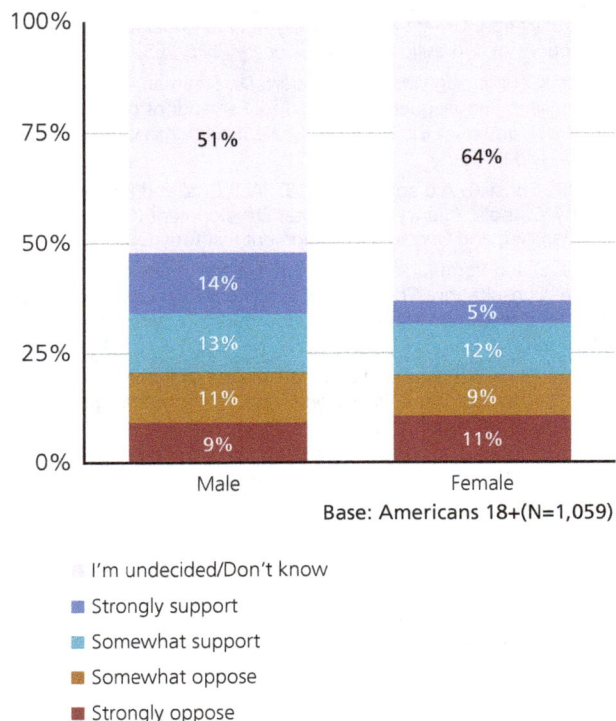

Base: Americans 18+(N=1,059)

- I'm undecided/Don't know
- Strongly support
- Somewhat support
- Somewhat oppose
- Strongly oppose

Source: Clarke et al. (2013)

- The negative gender and human rights impacts of large-scale renewable energy development should be avoided. From monoculture biomass plantations to hydropower dams, gender-equality safeguards and equal participation by women in all stages of the renewable energy cycle need to be ensured, including through monitoring, evaluation and verification schemes and participation by women's civil society organizations in these schemes.

- A foremost priority for all energy plans must be to enable safe and sustainable household energy. The creation of local renewable energy user groups and co-operatives, and empowerment of women to fully participate at all levels of decision-making, will be essential for sustainable success.

- Financial mechanisms need to be created; low-interest loans, start-up and capacity building grants, solidarity pricing mechanisms and specific access for women to funding should be developed.

- Policies, programmes and projects should equitably valorize women's and men's time and labour burdens and expenditures (UN Women 2016).

- Women should be recognized as independent users of energy solutions and enabled to benefit from energy access, taking into consideration the challenges of land ownership/rights, access to credit, and social constraints (UN Women 2016).

With increasingly rapid transition from finite to renewable energy sources, the risks of accidents could increase. Insurance and liability should become mandatory for the entire energy industry (including nuclear) to fully cover the costs of decommissioning, tailings clean-up and accidents, and compensation of direct and indirect victims. Free and affordable legal support should be made available to women and men in land rights, pollution and compensation cases.

For effective risk prevention and management in development projects, existing environmental and social safeguards need to be strengthened, including their gender components and ensuring compliance with these safeguards.

The planned increase in renewable small-grid and off-grid energy solutions has great potential to address the gendered face of energy poverty by reducing unpaid work burdens and increasing economic and personal development opportunities for women and men.

Increasingly, governments and the private sector are convinced of the need for greater parity in decision-making. A trend towards the presence of more women on boards and in government positions is expected to continue; however, technical areas such as the energy sector should be a specific focus.

Policy-makers need to recognize the importance of women in the energy sector and to engage them directly in policy-making and project design. Strengthening women's leadership and participation in sustainable energy solutions is critical in the transition to sustainable energy for all, and critical to reaching internationally agreed development goals (UN Women 2016).

References

Boudet, H., Clarke, C., Bugden, D., Maibach, E., Roser-Renouf, C. and Leiserowitz, A. (2014). 'Fracking' controversy and communication: Using national survey data to understand public perceptions of hydraulic fracturing, *Energy Policy*, 65, 57-67.

Brasier, K.J., McLaughlin, D.K., Rhubart, D., Stedman, R.C., Filteau, M.R. and Jacquet, J. (2013). Risk Perceptions of Natural Gas Development in the Marcellus Shale. *Environmental Practice*, 15(02), 108-122.

CAFOD, Christian Aid and ODI (2015) FAQ: Coal and Energy Poverty. Catholic Agency For Overseas Development (CAFOD), Christian Aid, and Overseas Development Institute (ODI).

Cotula, L. and Vermeulen, S. (2010). Over the Heads of Local People: Consultation, Consent and Recompense in Large-Scale Land Deals for Biofuels Projects in Africa. Journal of Peasant Studies, 37, 4, 899-916.

Cecelski, E. (2002). *Enabling Equitable Access to Rural Electrification: Current Thinking on Energy,* Poverty and Gender. ENERGIA, Washington, D.C.

Clarke, C. E., Boudet, H. S., and Bugden. D. (2013). Fracking in the American mind: Americans' views on hydraulic fracturing in September, 2012. Yale Project on Climate Change Communication., New Haven, CT.

Davis, C. and Fisk, J.M. (2014). Energy Abundance or Environmental Worries? Analyzing Public Support for Fracking in the United States, *Review of Policy Research*, 31(1), 1-16.

EIGE (2012) *Review of the implementation in the EU of area K of the Beijing Platform for Action : Women and the Environment* (978-92-9218-026-3). European Institute for Gender Equality.

Enerdata (2015). *Global Energy Statistical Yearbook 2015*. World Energy Consumption and Stats.

Finucane, M.L., Slovic, P., Mertz, C.K., Flynn, J. and Satterfield, T.A. (2000). Gender, race, and perceived risk: The 'white male' effect, *Health, Risk and Society*, 2(2), 159-172.

GACC (2013). *Scaling Adoption of Clean Cooking Solutions through Women's Empowerment:* A Resource Guide. Global Alliance For Clean Cookstoves.

Geere, J.A., Hunter, P.R. and Jagals, P. (2010). Domestic Water Carrying and Its Implications for Health: A Review and Mixed Methods Pilot Study in Limpopo Province, South Africa. *Environmental Health*, 9, 52

GCEC (2014). *The New Climate Economy.* The Global Commission on the Economy and Climate, London.

Gill, K., Patel, P., Kantor, P. and MacGonagle, A. (2012) *Invisible Market: Energy and Agricultural Technologies for Women's*

*Economic Advancement.*International Centre for Research on Women (ICRW), Washington, D.C.

Gustafson, P. (1998). Gender Differences in Risk Perception: Theoretical and Methodological Perspectives, *Risk Analysis,* 18(6), 805-811.

Hasham, N. (2015). More men back nuclear, women like solar: climate change gender divide found, *The Sidney Morning Herald.* [Online] Available at: http://www.smh.com.au/federal-politics/political-news/men-back-nuclear-women-like-solar-climate-change-gender-divide-found-20150809-giv5vk.html.

IEA (2014). *World Energy Outlook*

Skinner, J. (2016). Women pay heavier price for big dams. IIED, Blogs [Online] Available at: http://www.iied.org/women-pay-heavier-price-for-big-dams

ILO (1995). *Women Work More, But are Still Paid Less.* ILO.

ILO and EU (2011) *Investment in renewable energy generates jobs. Supply of skilled workforce needs to catch up.* ILO and EU.

Kahn Ribeiro, S., Kobayashi, S., Beuthe, M., Gasca, J., Greene, D., Lee, D. S., Muromachi, Y., Newton, P. J., Plotkin, S., Sperling, D., Wit, R., Zhou, P. J. (2007). Transport and its infrastructure, In *Climate Change 2007: Mitigation. Contribution of Working Group III to the Fourth Assessment Report of the IPCC* [B. Metz, O.R. Davidson, P.R. Bosch, R. Dave, L.A. Meyer (eds)], Cambridge University Press, Cambridge and New York.

Machol, B. and Rizk, S. (2013). Economic value of U.S. fossil fuel electricity health impacts, *Environment International,* 52, 75-80.

Matinga, N.M. (2010). *We grow up with it; An Ethnographic Study of the Experiences, Perceptions and Responses to the Health Impacts of Energy Acquisition and Use in Rural South Africa.* University of Twente, Enschede, the Netherlands.

Miralles-Guasch, C., Melo, M.M. and Marquet, O. (2015). A gender analysis of everyday mobility in urban and rural territories: from challenges to sustainability, *Gender, Place and Culture* 23.3, 398-417.

Newport, F. (2012). Americans Still Favor Nuclear Power a Year After Fukushima, *Gallup.* [Online] Available at: http://www.gallup.com/poll/153452/americans-favor-nuclear-power-year-fukushima.aspx.

OECD and IEA (2014). *Capturing the Multiple Benefits of Energy Efficiency.* International Energy Agency (IEA), OECD, Paris.

Populus (2011). British attitudes to new nuclear power stations. Available at: http://www.populus.co.uk/wp-content/uploads/download_pdf-250411-Financial-Times-British-attitudes-to-new-nuclear-power-stations.pdf

Prüss-Ustün, A., Wolf, J., Corvalán, C., Bos, R. and Neira, M. (2016). *Preventing disease through healthy environments: a global assessment of the burden of disease from environmental risks.* WHO, Geneva.

Pye, S. and Dobbin, A. (2015). Energy poverty and vulnerable consumers in the energy sector across the EU: analysis of policies and measures. *Insight_E.* Policy Report 2, May 2015.

REN21 (2015) Renewables 2015; *Global Status Report.* REN21, Paris.

REN21 (2013). Renewables 2013; *Global Status Report.* REN21 Secretariat, Paris.

Rojas, A., Perebble, M. and Siles, J. (2015). Flipping the Switch: Ensuring the energy sector is sustainable and gender-responsive. In *Roots for the future: The Landscape and Wayforward on Gender and Climate Change.* International Union for Conservation of Nature (IUCN), Global Gender and Climate Alliance (GGCA), Washington, DC.

Sacks, J.D., Stanek, L.W., Luben, T.J., Johns, D.O., Buckley, B.J., Brown, J.S. and Ross, M. (2011). 'Particulate matter-induced health effects: who is susceptible?', *Environment Health Perspective,* 119(4), 446-54.

SSP (2016). Swayam Shikshan Prayog: Empowering women as leaders and entrepreneurs [Online]. Available at: http://www.sspindia.org/?page_id=810

UN Women (2016). Progress of the World's Women 2015-2016 : *Transforming Economies, Realizing Rights.* UN Women, New York.

UNIDO and UN Women (2013). *Sustainable energy for all: the gender dimensions.* UNIDO and UN Women.

UNSD (2015). *The World's Women 2015: Trends and Statistics.* United Nations Statistics Division (UNSD), New York.

UNSD (2010). *The World's Women 2015: Trends and Statistics.* United Nations Statistics Division (UNSD), New York.

Villeneuve, P.J., Weichenthal, S.A., Crouse, D., Miller, A.B., To, T., Martin, R.V., van Donkelaar, A., Wall, C. and Burnett, R.T. (2015). Long-term Exposure to Fine Particulate Matter Air Pollution and Mortality Among Canadian Women, *Epidemiology,* 26(4), 536-45.

WHO (2015). *GHO: Household air pollution* [Online]. Available at: http://www.who.int/gho/phe/indoor_air_pollution/en/

WHO (2014). *WHO guidelines for indoor air quality: household fuel combustion.* WHO, Geneva.

WHO (2013). *Outdoor air pollution a leading environmental cause of cancer deaths.* WHO, Lyon, Geneva.

World Bank (2015). *Electric power consumption (kWh per capita).* Available at: http://data.worldbank.org/indicator/EG.USE.ELEC.KH.PC?order=wbapi_data_value_2012+wbapi_data_value+wbapi_data_value-lastand sort=asc .

World LP Gas Association (2014). *Cooking with Gas: Why women in developing countries want LPG and how they can get it.* Global Alliance for Clean Energia, Sustainable Energy for All.

Woroniuk, B. and Schalkwyk, J. (1998). Energy Policy and Equality between Women and Men. *Equality Prompt,* 9, SIDA, Stockholm.

Key Messages

- Households are seen as primary sites of consumption, but prevailing assumptions that women "control" household-based consumption choices oversimplify gender dynamics within households.

- Gendering of consumer goods is explicitly used as a tool to increase demand. From cars to cosmetics to recreational goods, notions of femininity and masculinity shape production and consumption decisions.

- Chronic exposure to now-ubiquitous plastics and industrial chemicals causes millions of deaths each year, and even more disease and disability. The health effects of such exposures are markedly gender-differentiated.

- Many developing countries rely on an economic growth strategy based on export-oriented industrial production. The economic benefits of these growth strategies are unevenly distributed, and pre-existing gender inequalities in wages are often used as a selling point to attract low-entry industrial investment.

- While women and men express considerable commitment to more sustainable futures, they have different levels of personal commitment to enabling transformations towards sustainability.

2.4

Types of consumption

The current global pace and trajectory of consumption and production are environmentally unsustainable and socially inequitable (WWF 2015, Hoekstra and Wiedmann 2014). Rapid economic growth and human development since the 1950s have come at a significant cost in terms of global environmental pressures and impacts. Over-consumption as a cultural norm, and as a conspicuous signifier of modernity and class status, is a defining characteristic in developed countries and is increasingly an aspirational signifier in middle-income and developing countries.

The resource depletion and environmental consequences of accelerated consumption and production are not evenly distributed globally (WWF 2014, FOE et al. 2009). Neither are they evenly distributed on smaller scales, including at the intra-household level. "Average" consumption rates hide significant gender and class differences at both the high and low ends of "average" consumption (Oxfam 2015, UNEP 2012, WHO 2010, Pellow 2007, Ringquist 2005). Inequalities occur along several social axes, with women facing greater risks than men, rural communities often more exposed than urban ones, and groups marginalized because of race, ethnicity or other factors likely to be disproportionately affected (Oxfam 2015). Poverty is an environmental threat-multiplier and, in most places, women are more likely than men to live in extreme poverty (UN 2015, UNDP 2015, USAID 2015, UNDP n.d.).

Consumption of plastics and chemicals

The types of materials consumed have changed dramatically in recent decades. From 1950 to 2012 global plastics growth averaged 8.7% per year, rising from 1.7 million tons to the nearly 300 million tons of 2015 (The Globalist 2015). Plastics and synthetic chemicals have become globally ubiquitous: once they have made their way into the air we breathe, the water we drink, and the food we eat, they also end up in our bodies. In the average human being, dozens of toxins have been identified through "body burden" analysis of samples of blood, the umbilical cord, the placenta, breast milk, urine, hair, sperm and fatty tissue, even among people who live in isolated regions of the worl (COPHES 2012, CDC 2009, Schuiling 2005). While many chemicals pose a constant risk, for both women and men there may be particular windows of susceptibility, especially during infancy and puberty and, for women, during pregnancy, when the impacts of chemical exposures can have critical health effects (WHO 2014, Kortenkamp et al. 2011).

In women increasing epidemiological evidence points to strong links between breast cancer and exposure to chemicals such as PCBs, organic solvents, DDT/DDE, BPA, PAHs, phenols, alkylphenols, phthalates, parabens, styrene, metals, phytoestrogens, chemicals in first or second-hand smoke, and heavy metals such as cadmium (WECF 2016, WHO and UNEP 2013, Kortenkamp 2008, Brody et al. 2007, Watts 2013, Lynn 2007, Murray et al. 2007). In men subfertile sperm counts are increasingly common; testicular cancer increased 400% over the last 50 years in industrialized countries and, by the early 2000s, was the most common cancer in men between 20 and 45 years old (WHO and UNEP 2013, Richiardi et al. 2004, Huyghe et al. 2003).

Households as sites of consumption

One approach to measuring the impacts of consumption is "ecological footprint" analysis, in which consumption is usually measured as end-user demand. Through the footprint lens, in most countries the household is positioned as the primary locus of consumption demand. Understanding the intra-household gender dynamics of consumption requires nuanced analysis.

There is little evidence to support the widespread assumption that being the "principal shopper" in the household means that women make the majority of decisions about household purchases. Taking on a shopping role does not necessarily imply that a woman has greater agency and autonomy in decision-making about consumption. Assumptions about women "controlling" household-based consumption choices often prove to be erroneous when micro-scale analysis is available.

Shining the environmental spotlight on unsustainable consumption is an important and necessary strategy for directing attention to the major drivers of global environmental degradation. But identifying "the household" as a primary site of that unsustainability has the distortive effect of placing global responsibility on feminized sites (households and individual consumer choices) while deflecting attention from masculinized constellations of unsustainable consumption such as militaries and extractive industries.

Structural factors in unsustainable consumption

Many large-scale social and economic forces drive unsustainable consumption and production, including:

Normative economic models: The assumption that production and consumption can and should continuously grow is at the heart of mainstream economics and its primary metric, GDP. Mainstream economic models presume that continuous growth is possible, even in closed systems such as the planet (UNEP 2015). Measuring economies through a GDP lens means all economic activity is counted as "good" regardless of the origins of such activities or the consequences. Among other ironies, this means environmental disasters may be considered to provide economic benefits due to the increased labour, materials and reconstruction spending in their aftermath. On the other hand, pollution, resource degradation and waste are not counted against GDP (Stiglitz *et al.* 2010).

GDP-based economic orthodoxy also reflects deeply gendered norms and assumptions about what counts as economic activity. GDP-based growth does not count most of the actual work done in an economy, nor "well-being". Feminist economists make the case that the contributions of most of the world's women are left out of the conventional global economic model: reproductive work, unpaid caring labour, unpaid household labour, child care, volunteer work, artisanal work that is not market-based, subsistence labour, bartering activities and informal activities (a large share of which are done by women) are completely invisible in conventional global and national accounts (Waring 1988). Women work three out of every four hours of unpaid labour, none of which is counted in GDP-based measurements (UNDP 2015).

Urbanization and consumption: The proportion of the world's population living in urban areas is expected to increase to 66% by 2050 (UN DESA 2014). If this growth follows business as usual (BAU) models, it will accelerate the growth of cities' ecological footprint (WWF 2014). City dwellers are consumers. Indeed, in most of the world it is the function of cities as centres of consumption that drives urban growth much more than their function as production centres (Poumanyvong and Kaneko 2010, Luque 2015). The shift to urban living is increasing the incomes of millions of people around the world. A billion people in cities will enter the global "consuming class" by 2025, with incomes high enough to become significant consumers of goods and services.

Growing income inequality is strongly associated overall with urbanization, especially in the most rapidly urbanizing settings (Ukhova 2015, Oxfam 2011). This income inequality is also highly associated with gender inequality. The emerging urban discretionary-income, consumption class is not equally populated by women and men, although much of the gender-specific effect is masked by the standard practice of collecting information on consumption and spending by "household" units. Men dominate the ranks of the rich, high-consuming urban class, especially at the top of the wealth pyramid. A recent IMF study examining the linkages of gender and income inequality revealed that, at the top of the income ladder, higher gender inequality is strongly associated with higher income shares in the top 10% income group (Gonzales 2015).

Driving consumer aspirations through advertising: Commercial marketing and advertising are powerful drivers of consumer aspirations. Advertising creates demand for consumer goods, even those for which there was previously limited or no demand; influences consumer choices; creates identification with brands; and shapes perceptions about the role of commodities and consumption in signifying personal identity, success and accomplishment. Linked to globalization trends and spreading developed world lifestyles, advertising is widely seen as a primary driver in spreading consumption patterns globally and fuelling excessive consumption in developed countries (Henderson 2012, World Federation of Advertisers 2002).

Gendering of commodities is explicitly used as a tool to increase demand for material goods. In addition to selling goods based on their gendered associations, marketers strive to embed gender identities within specific commodities that would otherwise have no innate sex-differentiated characteristics. Gendering consumer goods, or associating them exclusively with women or men, allows manufacturers to double their potential market: if marketers can successfully persuade women and men that they need gender-distinct deodorants, running shoes, toys, pens, watches, cars, soaps, skin creams or bicycles, among many other commodities, gender manipulation becomes a driver both of greater consumption and of gender-specialized production.

Norms of femininity and masculinity as high environmental impact consumption drivers: Norms of femininity and masculinity drive consumption of products. Among other globally significant examples of high environmental impact consumption, the

Box 4: Norms of masculinity and femininity as drivers of meat consumption

The environmental impacts of the beef industry globally are receiving increasing attention (UNEP-GEAS 2012, UNEP 2009, York and Gossard 2004). Global meat and dairy consumption is rising rapidly, closely associated with increases in urbanization and in individuals' purchasing power (FAO 2002, FAO n.d.).

Meat eating is closely gendered: meat is symbolically and socially associated with manhood (Wellesley *et al.* 2015; Adams 2010). It is a global pattern that men emphasize meat and women minimize it as part of their gender identity. Men are seen to "need" meat more than women. Its consumption is viewed as a male prerogative. Food taboos about eating meat are applied more often to women than men, and when poverty or food insecurity compel a deliberate restriction of the amount of meat consumed women eat it last and least (Rothgerber 2013, Sobal 2005, Leghorn and Roodkowsky 1977).

In the United States adult women eat about 20% less than adult men overall. However, they eat 44% less beef, 39% less pork and 23% less poultry (USDA 2012). In São Paolo, Brazil, the ratio is similar.

Daily meat consumption, United States, 2012, grams per day

	Beef	Pork	Poultry	Total
Men	78.16	38.07	61.53	177.76
Women	43.64	23.08	47.18	113.90

Daily beef and pork consumption, São Paolo, 2008, grams per day

Men	104.1
Women	59.4

Source: de Carvalho et al. (2014)

Most environmental analysts agree that changes in meat eating will be required for environmental sustainability. The social constructions of femininity and masculinity therefore need to be taken seriously in the policy arena in order to achieve a shift away from unsustainable patterns.

consumption of meat, cars and personal cosmetics are distinctly gendered. The GGEO provides case studies on meat, cars and cosmetics consumption to illustrate how unsustainable consumption is often deeply gendered, and intentionally so, in order to promote consumption **(Box 4)**.

Pointing out that meat, cars and cosmetics consumption presents gendered environmental problems does not mean *individual* women and men are responsible for these global problems or for their solutions. Such gender identities are constructed through a combination of complex social forces including large, profitable industrial and marketing structures. Identifying the gendering of unsustainable consumption means the social constructions of femininity and masculinity need to be taken seriously in the policy arena if a shift away from unsustainable patterns is to be achieved.

Production and waste

Unsustainable consumption is interwoven with unsustainable production. Production of material goods takes place in a sex-segregated and gender-discriminatory labour context, a pattern that plays out at local as well as global scales and in developing as well as developed countries.

Gender inequality and global production

Attracting transnational export-oriented production and industrialization investments has become a primary strategy for developing countries in order to improve their economies, reduce poverty and increase formal employment. Gender inequality stimulates growth as employers tap lower-wage women to work in industrial production to keep the costs of goods low for export (Seguino 2000, Ertürk and Çagatay 1995). As multinational companies scour the globe for ever-cheaper production sites, the fact that women's labour can usually be made cheaper than men's means women typically predominate on the bottom tier of most global production systems. The bottom tiers of global industrial production, often among the most feminized, are also among the most dangerous for workers.

The social costs, particularly the gender inequities, of export-oriented low-end production are paralleled by environmental damage (which, in turn, exacerbates social impacts). Catastrophic workplace accidents are not uncommon in emerging-economy industrial workplaces. The environmental impacts of globalized production in developing countries are extraordinarily high, including air and water pollution, chemical contamination and accidents associated with production sites. The synchronicity between social and environmental damage is not surprising since both are integral to the global industrialization strategy: environmental and gender inequalities converge in this sector of the modern global economy.

Waste

Most countries in the world face waste crises, particularly in urban areas. In most developing countries a high proportion of the waste produced is recycled through informal and sometimes illegal systems of waste picking. There are millions of waste pickers in the world, in many cases predominantly women and children, but in others mostly men or gender-mixed (Medina 2008, Chaturvedi 2010). Few data exist, and almost no gender-disaggregated data, on waste pickers and the waste-picking economy. One of the most hazardous wastes, especially for developing countries, is electronic and electrical waste ("e-waste"). Most e-waste is discarded in the general waste stream. Of the e-waste in developed countries sent for recycling, 80% ends up being shipped (often illegally) to developing countries (Lundgren 2012). The manual sorting, stripping, burning and recycling of e-waste and the hazards associated with it symbolize the global production and consumption crisis.

Transformational change – moving forward

Consistently and across national assessments, research findings point to gender differences (often at significant levels) in social and economic development, consumption patterns, access and use of knowledge, approach to environmental issues, ecological footprints, use, access and control of environmental resources, and management of the environment (ILO 2015, UN Women 2013). Glimpses of these differences suggest that women might be the more engaged demographic for bringing sustainability forward:

- A 2007 survey in the EU asked citizens whether they were willing to pay more to use less polluting system of transportation: 43% of men and 39% of women said they were not prepared to do so; 48% of women and 42% of men were willing to pay up to 10% more (Eurobarometer 2007).

- A meta-analysis of research on gender and environmental attitudes across 14 countries found a clear picture that women were consistently stronger in pro-environmental behaviour and attitudes (Zelezny *et al.* 2000).

- In Germany, recent studies establish that women are more likely to be conscious of and act on sustainable consumption than their male peers (Costa Pinto *et al.* 2014).

- A preliminary study in the United Arab Emirates in 2015 found women more focused on purchasing and consuming products that are environmentally friendly, and they were more aware of conserving energy and other natural resources compared to men (Kahn and Trivedi 2015).

Findings such as these point to the need to engage women as well as men in planning for a sustainable future. The emerging focus on developing a "green economy" provides an opportunity to address both environmental degradation and gender discrimination within economic frameworks. Without gender-informed guidance and policy intervention, however, a more "green" economy will do little to relieve gender inequalities and may exacerbate them to the detriment of overall sustainability (ILO 2015, UNRISD 2012, ENERGIA 2011).

References

Adams, C. (2010). *The sexual politics of meat: A feminist-vegetarian critical theory.* Aand C Black.

Brody, J.G., Moysich, K.B., Humblet, O., Attfield, K.R., Beehler, G.P. and Rudel, R.A. (2007). Environmental pollutants and breast cancer: epidemiologic studies, *Cancer,* 109 (12 Suppl), 2667-711.

CDC (2009). *Fourth National Report on Human Exposure to Environmental Chemicals.* CDC, Atlanta.

Chaturvedi, B. (2010). *Mainstreaming Waste Pickers and the Informal Recycling Sector in the Municipal Solid Waste.* Women in Informal Employment: Globalizing and Organizing (WIEGO).

COPHES (Consortium to Perform Human Biomonitoring on a European Scale) (2012). *Human Biomonitoring* [Online]. Available at: http://www.eu-hbm.info/cophes#sthash.7tv973Tj.dpuf%29

Costa Pinto, D., Herter, M.M., Rossi, P. and Borges, A. (2014). Going green for self or for others? Gender and identity salience effects on sustainable consumption, *International Journal of Consumer Studies,* 38(5), 540-549.

de Carvalho, A.M., Cesar, C.L., Fisberg, R.M. and Marchioni, D.M. (2014). Meat consumption in Sao Paulo-Brazil: trend in the last decade, *PLoS One,* 9(5), p. e96667.

ENERGIA/E.D.N./Global/Forest Coalition/ VAM/WOCAN/WEDO/ WECF (2011). A Gender Perspective on the 'Green Economy': Equitable, healthy and decent jobs and livelihoods. Women's Major Group position paper in preparation for the *United Nations Conference on Sustainable Development* 2012.

Ertürk, K. and Çagatay, N. (1995). Macroeconomic consequences of cyclical and secular changes in feminization: An experiment at gendered macromodeling, *World Development,* 23(11), 1969-1977.

Eurobarometer (2007). *Attitudes on Issues related to EU Transport policy.* Flash EB No206b – EU Transport Policy and The Gallup Organization.

FAO (2002). *World agriculture: Towards 2015/2030. Summary report.* FAO, Rome.

FAO (n.d.). Milk and milk products [Online]. Available at: http://www.fao.org/agriculture/dairy-gateway/milk-and-milk-products/en/#.V0HAp1dF_zJ

FOE., SERI and Global 2000 (2009). *Overconsumption?: Our use of the World's Natural Resources.* Sustainable Europe Research Institute (SERI), Austria and GLOBAL 2000 (Friends of the Earth Austria).

Gonzales, C., Sonali Jain-Chandra, Kalpana Kochhar, Monique Newiak, and Tlek Zeinullayev (2015). *Catalyst for Change: Empowering Women and Tackling Income Inequality.* IMF, Washington DC.

Hallegatte, S, Mook Bangalore, Laura Bonzanigo, Marianne Fay, Tamaro Kane, Ulf Narloch, Julie Rozenberg, David Treguer, and Adrien Vogt-Schilb (2016). *Shock Waves: Managing the Impacts of Climate Change on Poverty.* Climate Change and Development Series. World Bank, Washington, DC.

Henderson, H. (2012). Sustainable Consumption: A new role for advertising? *CSRWire Talkback.* [Online] Aavailable at: http://www.csrwire.com/blog/posts/602-sustainable-consumption-a-new-role-for-advertising

Hoekstra, A.Y. and Wiedmann, T.O. (2014). Humanity's unsustainable environmental footprint, *Science,* 344(6188), 1114-1117.

Huyghe, E., Matsuda, T. and Thonneau, P. (2003). Increasing incidence of testicular cancer worldwide: a review, *J Urol,* 170(1), 5-11.

ILO (2015) *Gender Eqaulity and Green Jobs.* International Labour Organization, http://www.ilo.org/wcmsp5/groups/public/---ed_emp/--emp_ent/documents/publication/wcms_360572.pdf.

Kahn, N and P. Trivedi (2015). Gender differences and Sustainable Consumption Behaviour. British Journal of Marketing Studies 3 (3), 29 – 35.

Kortenkamp, A. (2008). Breast cancer and exposure to hormonally active chemicals, An Appraisal of the Scientific Evidence. A background briefing paper.The School of Pharmacy, University of London.

Leghorn, L. and Roodkowsky, M. (1977). Who really starves?: Women and world hunger. Friendship Press, New York.

Lundgren, K. (2012). The global impact of e-waste: addressing the challenge. ILO, Geneva.

Luque, J. (2015). Urban Land Economics. Springer, Switzerland.

Lynn, H. (2007). Politics and prevention: Linking breast cancer and our environment. WECF.

Medina, M. (2008). The informal recycling sector in developing countries. GridLines

Murray, T.J., Maffini, M.V., Ucci, A.A., Sonnenschein, C. and Soto, A.M. (2007). Induction of mammary gland ductal hyperplasias and carcinoma in situ following fetal bisphenol A exposure, *Reprod Toxicol,* 23(3), 383-90.

Oxfam (2011). *Left behind by the G20? How inequality and environmental degradation threaten to exclude poor people from the benefits of economic growth.* Oxfam GB, Oxford.

Oxfam (2015). *Extreme Carbon Inequality* [Online]. Available at: https://www.oxfam.org/sites/www.oxfam.org/files/file_attachments/mb-extreme-carbon-inequality-021215-en.pdf

Pellow, D.N. (2007). *Resisting Global Toxics: Transnational Movements for Environmental Justice.* MIT Press.

Poumanyvong, P. and Kaneko, S. (2010). Does urbanization lead to less energy use and lower CO2 emissions? A cross-country analysis, *Ecological Economics,* 70(2), 434-444.

Prüss-Üstün A, J. Wolf, , C Corvalán, R Bos and M Neira. (2016). *Preventing disease through healthy environments: a global assessment of the burden of disease from environmental risks.* Geneva. WHO.

Richiardi, L., Bellocco, R., Adami, H.O., Torrang, A., Barlow, L., Hakulinen, T., Rahu, M., Stengrevics, A., Storm, H., Tretli, S. *et al.* (2004). Testicular cancer incidence in eight northern European countries: secular and recent trends, *Cancer Epidemiol Biomarkers Prev,* 13(12), 2157-66.

Ringquist, E.J. (2005). Assessing Evidence of Environmental Inequities: A Meta-Analysis, J*ournal of Policy Analysis and Management,* 24(2), 223-247.

Rothgerber, H. (2013). Real men don't eat (vegetable) quiche: Masculinity and the justification of meat consumption, Psychology of Men and Masculinity, 14(4), 363-375.

Saner, D. (2013). T*owards Sustainable Supply of Household Consumption: Demand Modeling and Environmental Assessment,* Zürich. Available at: http://e-collection.library.ethz.ch/eserv/eth:6793/eth-6793-02.pdf

Schuiling, J., and van der Naald, W. (2005). *A Present for Life: hazardous chemicals in umbilical cord blood.* Greenpeace Nederland and WWF.

Seguino, S. (2000). Gender Inequality and Economic Growth: A Cross-Country Analysis, *World Development,* 28(7), 1211-1230.

Sobal, J. (2005). Men, meat, and marriage: models of masculinity, *Food and Foodways,* 13(1-2), 135-158.

Stiglitz, J. E., Sen, A., and Fitoussi, J. P. (2010). *Mismeasuring our lives:* Why GDP doesn't add up. The New Press, New York.

The Globalist. (2015). The Rise of Plastic. [Online] http://www.theglobalist.com/the-rise-of-plastic/

Ukhova, D. (2015). Gender inequality and inter-household economic inequality in emerging economies: exploring the relationship, *Gender and Development,* 23(2), 241-259.

UN (2015). *The Millenium Development Goals Report 2015.* Summary.

UNDP. n.d., Gender and poverty reduction [Online]. Available at: http://www.undp.org/content/undp/en/home/ourwork/povertyreduction/focus_areas/focus_gender_and_poverty.html

UNDP (2015). *Human Development Report 2015.* UNDP, New York.

UNEP (2015). *Sustainable Consumption and Production: A Handbook for Policymakers.*

UNEP (2012). *GEO 5 Global Environmental Outlook: Environment for the Future We Want.* UNEP.

UNEP (2009) *The environmental food crisis – The environment's role in averting future food crises.* A UNEP rapid response assessment. United Nations Environment Programme, GRID-Arendal.

UN-DESA (2014). *World Urbanization Prospects.* 2014 Revision, Highlights.United Nations, Department of Economic and Social Affairs, Population Division.

UNEP-GEAS (2012). Growing greenhouse gas emissions due to meat production.

UNRISD (2012). *Gender in the Green economy.* Available at: http://www.unrisd.org/unrisd/website/newsview.nsf/%28httpNews%29/C9BAB159600EE0A5C1257A210036A71C?OpenDocument.

UN Women (2013). *A Transformative Stand-alone Goal on Achieving Gender Equality, Women's Rights and Women's Empowerment: Imperatives and Key Components.* UN Women, New York, USA.

USAID (2015). *Gender and Extreme Poverty.* https://www.usaid.gov/sites/default/files/documents/1870/Gender_Extreme_Poverty_Discussion_Paper.pdf

USDA (2012) *Commodity Consumption by Population Characteristics.*USDA/ Economic Research Service.

Waring, M. (1988). *If Women Counted: A New Feminist Economics.* Harper and Row, NY.

Watts, M.A. (2013). *Poisoning Our Future: Pesticides and Children.* Pesticide Action Network Asia and the Pacific.

WECF (2016). *Women and Chemicals: The impact of hazardous chemicals on women.*Women in Europe for a Common Future (WECF), http://www.wecf.eu/download/2016/March/WomenAndChemicals_PublicationIWD2016.pdf.

Wellesley, L., C. Happer, and A. Froggatt, (2015) Changing Climate, Changing Diets: *Pathways to Lower Meat Consumption Chatham House.*

WHO (2010). *Environment and health risks: a review of the influence and effects of social inequalities.*World Health Organization (WHO) Europe.

WHO (2014). *Global status report on noncommunicable diseases.* World Health Organization (WHO).

WHO and UNEP (2013). *State of the science of endocrine disrupting chemicals* - 2012. United Nations Environment Programme (UNEP) and World Health Organization (WHO).

World Federation of Advertisers (2002). *Industry as a partner for sustainable development: Advertising.*European Association of Communications Agencies (EACA), World Federation of Advertisers (WFA) and United Nations Environment Programme (UNEP).

WWF (2014). *Living Planet Report 2014.* World Wide Fund (WWF), Gland, Switzerland.

York, R. and Gossard, M.H. (2004). Cross-national meat and fish consumption: exploring the effects of modernization and ecological context, *Ecological Economics,* 48(3), 293-302.

Zelezny, L.C., Chua, P.-P. and Aldrich, C. (2000). New Ways of Thinking about Environmentalism: Elaborating on Gender Differences in Environmentalism, *Journal of Social Issues,* 56(3), 443-457.

MARINE AND COASTAL COMMUNITIES AND ECOSYSTEMS

Key Messages

- Women and men have common but differentiated responsibilities in the fishing sector. Fishing is frequently portrayed as a male domain, but when the entire fishing cycle is taken into account some 47% of the workforce is actually female.

- Fishing both reflects and defines gender boundaries; men are conventionally defined as "fishers" while women's activities in the sector are too often trivialized and overlooked in official programmes, data collection and support.

- Environmental change and damage to marine systems have gendered impacts, while women and men experience climate disruptions differently. Climate change is especially threatening to coastal communities and fishing livelihoods. "Downstream" effects on fishing sector activities such as post-harvest work are often not taken into account.

- Health impacts are gender-differentiated. For example, many marine contaminants are particularly dangerous for foetal development. Chemical contaminants in ocean systems bioaccumulate and threaten both human health and the health of marine organisms.

- As fisheries collapse globally and fish become scarce locally, many women have to turn to transactional sex to bridge the scarcity gap. Women's bodies are the shock absorbers of environmental and economic crises.

- Illegal, unreported and unregulated (IUU) fishing relies on trafficked, indentured and slave labour, mostly men.

- Evidence suggests that fisheries management improves when women are actively involved.

2.5

"What we take out": fish, fishing, identities and livelihoods

Some 35 million people in the world are fishers, 90% of whom are classified as small-scale fishers. Millions of other people take part in seasonal, occasional or informal fishing activities but may not be categorized as fishers in official statistics.

Open-ocean fishing is almost exclusively a male domain. Women predominate as fishers in coastal ecosystems, including mangroves, reefs, tidal flats and coastal estuaries, often gleaning and cultivating shellfish (Lambeth *et al.* 2014). This separation of activities is maintained through norms of femininity and masculinity: women's fishing work is often conceptualized as "not fishing", as if this work were an extension of their traditional role of (unpaid) household labour (SPC 2007). The association of fishing from boats, especially on open seas, with maleness is supported by cultural practices and taboos around the world with respect to women in boats (Lambeth *et al.* 2002, Williams *et al.* 2002).

Because male-identified capture fishing is considered "real" fishing, the entire fisheries sector is conventionally portrayed as a male enterprise (Willson 2014). Most official data focus on open-ocean fishing rather than the entire fishing cycle, which means women's contributions are largely hidden. The limited nature of gender-disaggregated databases on fisheries-related work makes it difficult to bring gender into relevant decision-making and policy platforms. Failure to fully account for participation in fishing activities by women and men has serious implications for fisheries management.

Women make up 47% of the total global fisheries workforce when all parts of the fishing cycle are counted (World Bank 2012), **(Table 3)**. They play a variety of roles in the fishery value chain in both large-scale and small-scale fisheries, and in both developed and developing countries, including post-harvest processing, selling, net-building, and myriad related tasks.

Above all, women are responsible for household nutritional security; in this role they are purchasers and consumers of fish, as well as fish sellers or traders. While roles and responsibilities within the fishing sector vary from one location to another, women's roles in providing nutritional security for their households remain relatively constant globally (Harper *et al.* 2013).

Women work in disproportionate numbers in fish processing factories.
Photo credit: © Sportsmens Cannery

Table 3: Global capture fisheries employment by gender

	Small-scale fisheries			Large-scale fisheries			Total
	Marine	Inland	Total	Marine	Inland	Total	
Number of fishers (millions)	13	18	31	2	1	3	34
Number of post-harvest jobs (millions)	37	38	75	7	0.5	7.5	82.5
Total	50	56	106	9	1.5	10.5	116.5
Percentage of women	36%	54%	46%	66%	28%	62%	47%

Source: World Bank (2012)

Illegal, unreported and unregulated fishing: Illegal, unregulated and unreported (IUU) fishing is a serious global problem that results in illegal harvests of millions of tonnes of fish and billions of dollars in revenues lost to legitimate fishers. IUU fishing threatens the health of fish populations and marine and coastal ecosystems worldwide, as well as the livelihoods and food security of millions of inhabitants of coastal areas (Hall 2016, Pew Charitable Trusts 2016). An estimated 14-33% of the total global catch consists of IUU fishing, with a value of US$8-19 billion (Borit and Olsen 2012). The IUU fishing industry is responsible for severe labour and human rights abuses. When IUU is carried out on an industrial scale on the open seas, it relies almost exclusively on labour by men, many of whom have been pressed into indentured labour and held on ships as actual or de facto slaves, often for years without being allowed off the ship (Urbina 2015, ILO 2013). Pirate fishing operations in particular are characterized by some of the worst working conditions and there are extensive reports of abuse. Women and girls have reportedly been subjected to human trafficking and forced labour on board these vessels, primarily for sexual exploitation rather than as fishing labourers. Women are also reported to be victims of trafficking in the land-based fish processing sector (ILO 2013).

In many communities around the world traditional fishing may suddenly be redefined as "IUU" if fishing access rights are taken away by governments, often in favour of larger fishing operations or for conservation reserves (Coope SoliDar R.L/ICSF in press 2016, Madrigal-Cordero and Solis-Rivera 2012). Already-marginalized groups, including women, are especially vulnerable to "ocean grabbing"; moreover, women fishers and gleaners whose work is concentrated in the foreshore and reef areas are often within sight of communities and open to surveillance and regulation for IUU "violations" in ways that other fishing is not (Bennet et al. 2015).

Post-harvest activities in the informal and formal sectors: In addition to women's heavy presence in fish extractive processes, they are closely associated with post-production processing and selling of fish (World Bank 2012). They have primary responsibilities in many countries for performing jobs such as smoking, salting and drying, as well as for selling fish and seafood products in local markets.

Women work in disproportionate numbers in seafood processing factories, preferentially hired due to the stereotype of women having "nimble hands" (for cleaning and gutting fish), and also because they cannot typically command as high wages as men (Hamilton *et al.* 2011). In Fiji women make up 90% of cannery workers (Lambeth *et al.* 2002); in South Africa 62% of the seafood processing workforce is female (Jeebhay *et al.* 2004); in Cambodia 80% of fish sauce factory workers are women (Dugan *et al.* 2010), while women make up over 90% of shrimp processors in India (Dhanya 2013).

Offshore oil, mining and seabed extraction: Extractive industries potentially provide development opportunities for communities, even when they operate offshore. While extractive industries such as near-shore oil production create jobs, these jobs mostly go to men. For millions of people in the world the reality is that these industries rarely benefit most communities in any significant way and are often destructive, disrupting the social fabric, depleting natural resources that are necessary for survival, and increasing health burdens in already vulnerable households **(Box 5)**. Women feel distinctive effects from extractive industries, particularly when the industry involves large numbers of transient non-local male labourers in small coastal communities (Scott *et al.* 2013). As these communities grow up around extractive industries, criminal networks are also likely to grow. For example, in Equatorial Guinea

trafficking of children and women for domestic and sexual exploitation in association with these industries increased dramatically (United States Department of State 2011).

"What we put in": contaminants and pollutants

Oil spills: Assessments of damage from oil spills usually focus on destruction caused to fisheries and to the livelihoods of men in the fishing industry; downstream impacts such as loss of fish processing jobs and ancillary businesses (often women's domains) that depend on robust fisheries are seldom counted as "fishing" impacts and are seldom compensated if oil companies are compelled to pay for losses (Olujide 2006).

Plastics: Plastic materials are now considered the most persistent and problematic type of marine debris, with widespread ecological and marine animal effects. Between 4.8 and 12.7 million tonnes of plastic debris per year enters the ocean (Jambeck *et al.* 2015). The fact that plastics persist for very long periods and are largely insoluble has significant implications for human health (Roy *et al.* 2011).

Box 5: Women's protests against seabed mining

Perhaps women's most prominent role in regard to seabed mining and other extractive processes is that of organized protest. Globally women have led efforts to prevent seabed mining. For example, the Vanuatu National Council of Women has insisted on the need to protect the seabed as an inherent foundation of wealth. At the 2012 UN Conference on Sustainable Development (Rio+20) women led a campaign to end experimental seabed mining (Hunter and Taylor 2013). On a remote island of Papua New Guinea women led efforts which succeeded in the gathering of 24,000 signatures to present to the government protesting experimental seabed mining (Jameson 2013).

Because of spatial differences in fishing by women and men, there may be significant gender differences in their experience, knowledge and impacts of marine plastics pollution. The build-up of plastic debris in coastal zones is severe and different in character from open-sea plastic pollution, with different impacts on women's near-shore fishing than on open-ocean fishing by men. Loss of economic activities, damage to well-being, and mental health aspects of the impacts of degraded environments are all gender-differentiated and likely to be more intense for women in near-shore fisheries than for men in those offshore. However, virtually no research or data exist on such differences.

Recent studies estimate that 263 tonnes of microbeads per year are released to the environment in the United States alone, about half of which pollute marine systems (Gouin *et al.* 2011). Microbeads were introduced in consumer goods to increase sales of personal care products. These products are among the most gender-manipulated consumer items, and the rapid proliferation of microbeads in them can only be understood as part of a gender-consumption nexus (UNEP and WECF in press). Women are socialized to be much heavier users of personal cosmetics than men. As heavy consumers of products containing microbeads, women have an opportunity and a responsibility to challenge the use of microbead products. The Plastic Soup Foundation, a women-led organization in the Netherlands, has taken the lead in organizing an international campaign against cosmetics-based maritime microbeads pollution, "Beat the Microbead", as has the 5 Gyres organization based in the United States (Plastic Soup Foundation, n.d.; 5 Gyres, n.d.).

Polychlorinated biphenyls (PCBs): PCBs are among the major bioaccumulating chemicals. They are found throughout the world's oceans, often at very high levels. PCBs are carried into marine systems by runoff from land-based industrial processes or through airborne deposits. They persist for many years in sediment deposits and in the food chain. In humans exposure to (or ingestion of) PCBs can damage the immune system, liver, skin, reproductive system, gastrointestinal tract and thyroid gland (Secretariat of the Stockholm Convention 2008); thyroid effects show differential impacts on women, men, boys and girls (Persky *et al.* 2001). Women are often advised to reduce or temporarily eliminate fish consumption during pregnancy to avoid transfer of ingested toxins to the foetus; in the case of PCBs this is ineffective in reducing both pre- and post-natal exposures, as they persist in the body for long periods and children are exposed to PCBs through breastfeeding and weaning foods (Binnington *et al.* 2014).

Methyl mercury: Methyl mercury is a heavy metal found in large quantities in marine systems. It is derived primarily from land-based industrial emissions, coal burning and mining processes. In the northern hemisphere ocean currents tend to drive methyl mercury contamination northward towards the Arctic, where it becomes further concentrated in large marine mammals. Some of the highest human concentrations have been found in indigenous children (especially those still breastfeeding) in the Canadian Arctic and northern Greenland, in populations that still depend heavily on seafood for sustenance (El-Hayak 2007).

Coastal communities change, insecurity and well-being: Small-scale fishing communities tend to be marginalized in social, economic, political and often geographical terms and often lack representation at the national or regional levels (Ratner *et al.* 2014). Cross-cultural research on poverty and fishing communities reveals a number of gendered vulnerabilities: income and assets in fishing communities are unevenly distributed between women and men, and incomes are highly variable in relationship to people's roles in the community and over time; both female and male fishers are often excluded from other income-earning opportunities, social services and political representation; and these fishers are exposed to higher than average levels of risk because they are marginalized and have a limited ability to cope with shocks due to resources collapse, climate change or changing social dynamics (Allison *et al.* 2012). Women are marginalized in distinctive ways, within already marginalized communities, with inequalities stemming from differences in identity, roles, relationships with respect to the marketplace, and household dynamics that affect asset accumulation, market opportunities, social capital and social norms (Thorpe *et al.* 2014, Béné and Merten 2008, Sen 2000).

When fisheries collapse, as is happening in many parts of the world, there is increasing documentation of women undertaking transactional sex to compensate for lost income associated with erratic or declining fish stocks (Neis *et al.* 2013) **(Box 6)**.

Impacts of climate change: Sea level rise, flooding, erosion and other impacts of climate change are already displacing millions of people globally (IPCC 2014). Sea level rise is particularly problematic for coastal communities. Not only does it result in loss of land, but also in contamination of near-shore water sources, increased erosion, and increased exposure to violent storms and wave surges. These impacts translate into lost livelihoods, property damage, forced migration and human rights violations.

The number of people forced to migrate from coastal regions is expected to increase dramatically due to climate change: 187 million could be displaced by 2100 (Nicholls *et al.* 2010). Low-lying coastal plains, deltas and small islands are especially susceptible to environmental migration (McLeman and Hunter 2010). Fishing communities may be affected by climate-induced migration caused by sea level rise, increasingly violent storms, and islands exposed to multiple climatic stresses and shocks (Islam *et al.* 2014). Gender and age play key roles regarding the ability to migrate, as well as influencing the outcomes of migration. Studies of coastal communities in Bangladesh have shown that older people and female heads of households are often less able to migrate because of cultural restrictions and limited income-earning opportunities both at home and in destination communities (Islam *et al.* 2014).

Changing climate conditions trigger not only human migration but also that of animals. Distribution patterns for fish, mammals and other species change in response to changing physical and biological components of ecosystems, such as water temperatures, food availability and water salinity. This has implications for the incomes, food security and migration patterns of human populations. Arctic communities are experiencing forced diet changes with shifts in the distribution patterns of marine mammals and fish, making access to traditional foods more difficult. In tropical zones the health of inshore fisheries, where women predominate, is especially dependent on the integrity of reef systems and seagrass ecosystems - highly threatened by climate change - to keep the fisheries intact.

Box 6: Bargaining power and sex in the context of declining fish catch

Gendered economies with highly skewed compensation frameworks (in which men have the capacity to earn much more money than women) affect the economic realities of gender relationships and the structure of intimate relationships within communities, including the development of sexual economies (Campbell 1997). Fishing economies have a highly gendered structure, with men often fishing while women process and sell the fish. However, the ways in which fish move from male fishing activities to women's processing and marketing vary considerably: in Sri Lanka many husbands and wives work as a team, with the man fishing and the wife selling; in Sierra Leone wives typically buy fish from their husbands in a business-like arrangement; in coastal Kenyan communities and other parts of Africa, fishermen give preferential access to women with whom they are in a sexual relationship.

Fish may be traded for sex where catches are declining.
Photo credit: © Habil Onyango - The Star

A study of fish workers in Zambia (Béné and Merten 2008) reported that 31% of fish traders had an institutionalized fish-for-sex relationship. In some cases these sexual transactions may be voluntary, but fishermen are frequently in stronger positions than fish traders both socially and economically. In the absence of money and other resources, female fish traders often lack the bargaining power to refuse a sexual relationship, either because of blackmail ("no sex, no fish") or because they cannot afford to turn down a favourable offer from a fisherman (Lwenya and Yongo 2012, Béné and Merten 2008). They also have unequal ability to negotiate safe sexual practices (Halperin and Epstein 2004). These fish-for-sex dynamics drive high HIV risk and prevalence rates, typically higher in fishing communities than elsewhere in countries with high overall prevalence rates, averaging four to 14 times above national averages (MacPherson *et al.* 2012, Allison and Seeley 2004, Entz *et al.* 2000). In addition to overall rates exceeding national averages, women in fishing communities frequently have higher rates of infection than men. One of the key drivers of HIV in fishing communities is fishing-related transactional sex and the unequal power and influence of women and girls in sexual relations means they are at special risk of infection (MacPherson *et al.* 2012).

Towards sustainability

The Small Island Developing States Network (SIDSnet), representing countries particularly threatened by climate change, has long been in the forefront of climate change activism and negotiation. Women in SIDS have been prominent in climate change activism and ocean protection efforts. Because of their vulnerability to sea level rise and the impacts of increased natural disasters, these countries were among the first to reject the global consensus of attempting to keep average global warming below the 2°C target, pressing for a maximum increase of 1.5°C above pre-industrial levels. In 2015 a global aspiration to limit this increase to 1.5°C was included in the Paris Agreement (UNFCCC 2015).

From community to national levels, strategies and policies that define rights and responsibilities in the fisheries sector have to contend with endemic problems such as inequitable access to and control over resources, conflict within communities, unsustainable resource use, and weak participation of significant stakeholders such as the poor and women (Leisher 2016, Agarwal 2010). Women often use natural resources differently than men, yet they frequently have minimal influence on how local resources are managed. Evidence from South Asia, including a meta-analysis of community fisheries management, reveals that empowering more women in local fisheries decision-making leads to better resource governance and conservation and increases women's social capital (Leisher 2016, Sultana *et al.* 2002).

Community-based women's groups around the world are in the forefront in developing gender-sensitive policy agendas that protect marine livelihoods and ecosystems, while at the same time promoting gender equality. Small-scale fisheries not only provide livelihoods, but also represent ways of life in which women's traditional knowledge and cultural identity have a prominence rarely found elsewhere (Begossi 2010).

References

5Gyres (n.d.) What we do [Website]. http://www.5gyres.org/what-we-do/

Agarwal B. (2010). *Gender and green governance: the political economy of women's presence.* Oxford University Press, Oxford.

Allison, E.H., Ratner, B.D., Åsgård, B., Willmann, R., Pomeroy, R. and Kurien, J. (2012). Rights-based fisheries governance: from fishing rights to human rights, Fish and Fisheries, 13(1), 14-29.

Allison, E.H. and Seeley, J.A. (2004). HIV and AIDS among fisherfolk: a threat to 'responsible fisheries'?, *Fish and Fisheries,* 5(3), 215-234.

Begossi, A. (2010). Small-scale fisheries in Latin America: management models and challenges. *MAST,* 9(2), 7-31.

Béné, C. and Merten, S. (2008). Women and Fish-for-Sex: Transactional Sex, HIV/AIDS and Gender in African Fisheries, *World Development,* 36(5), 875-899.

Bennett, N. J., Govan, H., and Satterfield, T. (2015). Ocean grabbing. *Marine Policy,* 57, 61–68.

Binnington, M.J., Quinn, C.L., McLachlan, M.S. and Wania, F. (2014). Evaluating the Effectiveness of Fish Consumption Advisories: Modeling Prenatal, Postnatal, and Childhood Exposures to Persistent Organic Pollutants, *Environmental Health Perspectives,* 122, 178–186.

Borit, M. and Olsen, P. (2012). Evaluation framework for regulatory requirements related to data recording and traceability designed to prevent illegal, unreported and unregulated fishing, *Marine Policy,* 36(1), 96-102.

Campbell, C. (1997). Migrancy, masculine identities and AIDS: the psychosocial context of HIV transmission on the South African gold mines, *Social Science and Medicine,* 45(2), 273-281.

Coope SoliDar R.L./ ICSF 2015-2016. (Forthcoming 2016). *Small scale fishing in Central American Indigenous People: Governance, tenure, and sustainable management of marine resources.* Chennai, India.

Dhanya, G. (2013). Status of women employed in seafood pre-processing units of Aiapuziia, Kerala, *Fishing Chimes,* 33(7).

Dugan, P., Delaporte, A., Andrew, N., O'Keefe, M. and Welcomme, R. (2010). B*lue Harvest: Inland Fisheries as an Ecosystem Service.* UNEP, Nairobi.

El-Hayek, Y. H. (2007). Mercury contamination in Arctic Canada: possible implications for Aboriginal health. *Journal of Developmental Disability,* 13, 67-89.

Entz, A.T., Ruffolo, V.P., Chinveschakitvanich, V., Soskolne, V. and Van Griensven, G.J.P. (2000). HIV-1 prevalence, HIV-1 subtypes and risk factors among fishermen in the Gulf of Thailand and the Andaman Sea, *AIDS,* 1027-1034.

Gouin, T., Roche, N., Lohmann, R. and Hodges, G. (2011). A thermodynamic approach for assessing the environmental exposure of chemicals absorbed to microplastic, E*nvironmental Science and Technology,* 45(4), 1466–1472.

Hall, R. (2016). Combating Illegal, Unreported, and Unregulated Fishing in #OurOcean, United States Department of State (Blog), 3 March 2016, https://blogs.state.gov/stories/2016/02/10/combating-illegal-unreported-and-unregulated-fishing-ourocean#sthash.bh7BeYy8.dpuf

Halperin, D.T. and Epstein, H. (2004). Concurrent sexual partnerships help to explain Africa's high HIV prevalence: implications for prevention, *The Lancet,* 364(9428), 4-6.

Hamilton, A., Lewis, A., McCoy, M.A., Havice, E. and Campling, L. (2011). *Market and Industry Dynamics in the Global Tuna Supply Chain.* Forum Fisheries Agency.

Harper, S., Zeller, D., Hauzer, M., Pauly, D. and Sumaila, U.R. (2013). Women and fisheries: Contribution to food security and local economies, *Marine Policy,* 39, 56-63.

Hunter, T. and Taylor, M. (2013). D*eep Sea Bed Mining in the South Pacific: A Background Paper.*The University of Queensland, Brisabane. Available at: http://www.law.uq.edu.au/documents/cimel/Deep-Sea-Bed-Mining-in-the-South-Pacific.pdf.

ILO (2013). *Caught at Sea. Forced labour and trafficking in fisheries.* http://www.ilo.org/wcmsp5/groups/public/--ed_norm/declaration/documents/publication/wcms_214472.pdf

IPCC (2014). *Climate Change 2014: Impacts, Adaptation and Vulnerability. Contribution of Working group II to the Fifth Assessment Report of the Intergovernmental Panel on Climate Change.* Cambridge University Press, New York.

Islam, M.M., Sallu, S., Hubacek, K. and Paavola, J. (2014). Migrating to tackle climate variability and change? Insights from coastal fishing communities in Bangladesh, *Climate Change* 124(4), 733-746.

Jambeck, J.R., Geyer, R., Wilcox, C., Siegler, T.R., Perryman, M., Andrady, A., Narayan, R. and Law, K.L. (2015). Plastic waste inputs from land into the ocean, *Science,* 347(6223), 768-771.

Jameson, A. (2013). Nautilus yu Nauti-lusman, *Papua New Guinea* Mine Watch. [Online] Available at: https://ramumine.wordpress.com/2013/06/24/nautilus-yu-nauti-lusman/.

Jeebhay, M.F., Robins, T.G. and Lopata, A.L. (2004). World at work: Fish processing workers, *Occupational and Environmental Medicine*, 61(5), 471-474.

Lambeth, L., Hanchard, B., Aslin, H., Fay-Sauni, L., Tuara, P., Rochers, K.D. and Vunisea, A. (2014). *An Overview of the Involvement of Women in Fisheries Activities in Oceania.*Secretariat of the Pacific Community, Noumea.

Lambeth, L., Hanchard, B., Aslin, H., Fay-Sauni, L., Tuara, P., Rochers, K.D. and Vunisea, A. (2002). An Overview of the Involvement of Women in Fisheries Activities in Oceania. In *Global symposium on women in fisheries.* The World Fish Center, Penang.

Lambeth, L. (2000). *An Assessment of the Role of Women within Fishing Communities in Tuvalu.* Secretariat of the Pacific Community, Noumea.

Leisher, C., Temsah, G., Booker, F., Day, M., Agarwal, B., Matthews, E., Roe, D., Russell, D., Samberg, L., Sunderland, T.C.H., Wilkie, D. (2016). Does the gender composition of forest and fishery management groups affect resource governance and conservation outcomes? A systematic map, *Environmental Evidence* 5:6

Lwenya, C. and Yongo, E. (2012). The fisherman's wife: vulnerabilities and strategies in the local economy; the case of lake Victoria, Kenya, *Signs,* 37(3), 566-573.

MacPherson, Eleanor E., John Sadalaki, Macdonald Njoloma, Victoria Nyongopa, Lawrence Nkhwazi, Victor Mwapasa, David G. Lalloo, Nicola Desmond, Janet Seeley, and Sally Theobald (2012). Transactional sex and HIV: understanding the gendered structural drivers of HIV in fishing communities in Southern Malawi, *Journal of the International AIDS Society* 15, no. 3.

Madrigal Cordero, P. and Solís Rivera, V. (2012). *Recognition and Support of ICCAs in Costa Rica.* In: Kothari, A. with Corrigan, C., Jonas, H., Neumann, A., and Shrumm, H. (eds). R*ecognising and Supporting Territories and Areas Conserved By Indigenous Peoples And Local Communities: Global Overview and National Case Studies.* Secretariat of the Convention on Biological Diversity, ICCA Consortium, Kalpavriksh, and Natural Justice, Montreal, Canada. Technical Series no. 64.

McLeman, R.A. and Hunter, L.M. (2010). Migration in the context of vulnerability and adaptation to climate change: insights from analogues, *Wiley interdisciplinary reviews. Climate change,* 1(3), 450-461.

Mills, D.J., Westlund, L., Graaf, G.D., Kura, Y., Willman, R. and Kelleher, K. (2011). Under-reported and undervalued: small-scale fisheries in the developing world. In *Small-scale fisheries management: frameworks and approaches for the developing world*. Eds. R.S. Pomeroy and N.L. Andrew. World Fish Center, Penang.

Neis, B., Gerrard, S. and Power, N. (2013). Women and children first: the gendered and generational social-ecology of smaller-scale fisheries in Newfoundland and Labrador and northern Norway, *Ecology and Society*, 18(4).

Nicholls, R.J., Marinova, N., Lowe, J.A., Brown, S., Vellinga, P., de Gusmão, D., Hinkel, J. and Tol, R.S.J. (2010). Sea-level rise and its possible impacts given a 'beyond 4°C world' in the twenty-first century, *Philosophical Transactions of the Royal Society of London A: Mathematical, Physical and Engineering Sciences*, 369(1934), 161-181.

Olujide, M.G. (2006). Perceived effect of oil spillage on the livelihood activities of women in Eastern Obolo local government area of Akwa Ibom State, *Journal of Human Ecology*, 19(4), 259-266.

Persky, V., Turyk, M., Anderson, H.A., Hanrahan, L.P., Falk, C., Steenport, D.N., Chatterton, R., Freels, S. and Great Lakes, C. (2001). The effects of PCB exposure and fish consumption on endogenous hormones, *Environmental Health Perspectives*, 109(12), 1275-1283.

Pew Charitable Trusts (2016). Ending Illegal Fishing 2016: Efforts Build on Earlier Gains, 3 March 2016, http://www.pewtrusts.org/en/research-and-analysis/analysis/2016/03/03/ending-illegal-fishing-2016-efforts-build-on-earlier-gains?hdand utm_campaign=2016-03-17%20Latestand utm_medium=emailand utm_source=Eloqua

Plastic Soup Foundation (n.d.). International Campaign Against Microbeads in Cosmetics [Website]. http://www.beatthemicrobead.org/en/industry

Ratner, B.D., Mam, K. and Halpern, G. (2014). Collaborating for resilience: conflict, collective action, and transformation on Cambodia's Tonle Sap Lake, *Ecology and Society*, 19(3).

Roy, P.K., Hakkarainen, M., Varma, I.K. and Albertsson, A.-C. (2011). Degradable polyethylene: fantasy or reality', *Environmental Science and Technology*, 45(10), 4217-4227.

Scott, J., Dakin, R., Heller, K. and Eftimie, A. (2013). *Extracting Lessons on Gender in the Oil and Gas Sector*. The World Bank, Washington DC.

(SPC) Secretariat for the Pacific Community (2007). *Women in Fisheries Information Bulletin* (1028-7752). Secretariat for the Pacific Community.

Secretariat of the Stockholm Convention (2008). PCBs Overview [Online]. Available at: http://chm.pops.int/Implementation/PCBs/Overview/tabid/273/Default.aspx.

Sen, A. (2000). Social Exclusion: Concept, Application and Scrutiny, *Office of Environment and Social Development, Asian Development Bank, Social Development Papers*, 1..

Sultana, P., Thompson, P. M., and Ahmed, M. (2002). Women-led fisheries management–a case study from Bangladesh. *Women in fisheries: pointers for development*, 89.

Thorpe, A., Pouw, N., Baio, A., Sandi, R., Ndomahina, E. and Lebbie, T. (2014). Fishing na everybody business": women's work and gender relations in Sierra Leone's fisheries, *Feminist Economics*, 20(3), 53-77.

UNEP and WECF (2016 in press). *Gender and Plastic*. UNEP, Nairobi.

UNFCCC (2015). Conference of the parties: adoption of the Paris Agreement. Available at: https://unfccc.int/resource/docs/2015/cop21/eng/l09r01.pdf.

United States Department of State (2011). *Trafficking in Persons Report - Equatorial Guinea*. Office to Monitor and Combat Trafficking in Persons, Washington, D.C.

Urbina, I. (2015). Sea slaves: The human misery that feeds pets and livestock, *The New York Times*. [Online] Available at: http://www.nytimes.com/2015/07/27/world/outlaw-ocean-thailand-fishing-sea-slaves-pets.html.

Williams, M.J., Chao, N.H., Choo, P.S., Matics, K., Nandeesha, M.C., Shariff, M., Siason, I., Tech, E. and Wong, J.M.C. (2002). Global Symposium on Women in Fisheries, *Sixth Asian Fisheries Forum*. Kaohsiung, Taiwan.

Willson, M.E. (2014). Icelandic fisher women's experience: Implications, social change, and fisheries policy, Ethnos, 79(4), pp. 525-550.

World Bank (2012). *Hidden Harvest: The Global Contribution of Capture Fisheries (66469-GLB)*. World Bank, Washington, D.C.

FORESTS AND FOREST ECOSYSTEMS

Key Messages

- Traditionally, forests are important to many people's daily lives and livelihood activities. They provide timber (e.g. for construction and furniture materials) and many other products (e.g. food, medicinal plants, fodder, colours for dying, fuelwood) as well as invaluable ecosystem services. Women and men in forest-dependent communities have different roles and purposes in traditional forest utilization.

- There is a well-documented gender gap in access to forest resources. Women often have less access to and control over forest land and resources than men (due to customary laws and social norms). The problem of unequal rights and access has been made worse by increasing forest over-exploitation for commercial purposes, including through land grabbing, logging and illegal wildlife trade.

- Land grabs and unsustainable mining projects have negative direct and indirect impacts on health and the environment, particularly with respect to poor and indigenous people (e.g. through lead and methylmercury contamination of soils and water resources and direct contact with toxic or harmful materials at mining sites). These negative impacts, which have large implications in regard to economic loss, are experienced differently by women and girls, men and boys.

- Illegal wildlife poaching and trade is a highly gendered conservation issue. Women and men tend to have different roles in the value chain, which includes hunting, processing, transporting, purchasing and consumption. Gender-specific studies and other information regarding gender and the wildlife trade, are nevertheless very limited.

- There are potential win-win relationships between more inclusive community forestry institutions, and better forest conditions and distributional equity. Women can play effective roles in formal forest protection forces, including combating illegal wildlife poaching and logging; however, adding environmentally related tasks to women's productive and reproductive responsibilities without considering social structures and norms (as well as the economic pressures associated with these resources) may overburden them.

2.6

Forest resources: supporting lives and livelihoods

Gender roles in forest utilization

The total number of forest-dependent people in the world is difficult to ascertain and the meaning of the term "forest dependent" can vary considerably from one location to another (Chao 2012, FAO n.d.). How the resources on which these people depend for their survival are obtained and used, by women and men, is largely determined by local contexts and customs. Women's knowledge and needs frequently differ from those of men, but similar patterns exist in different parts of the world. For example, timber extraction for household and community construction is often carried out mostly by men (especially in developing countries) while more complex gender roles are identifiable in the collection of non-timber forest products (NTFPs). Poor management or even loss of forest ecosystems can have different impacts on women than on men (Djoudi *et al.* 2015, WWF 2012, Aguilar *et al.* 2011).

Women and men collect NTFPs for household consumption and for their commercial value. NTFPs for household consumption are extremely important to people who are very poor. Trading them can provide a "safety net" to help respond to environmental and economic shocks (Wunder *et al.* 2014, Marshall *et al.* 2006). Both women and men generally collect NTFPs for both household consumption and commercial value; however, as shown in **Figure 5** the pattern of their roles is not globally consistent. Where there are lower collection rates for women than for men, the reasons can include limited forest access, market information and transport (Azzez *et al.* 2014, Sunderland *et al.* 2014).

Figure 5: Shares of unprocessed forest products collected by women, men and both at global and regional levels

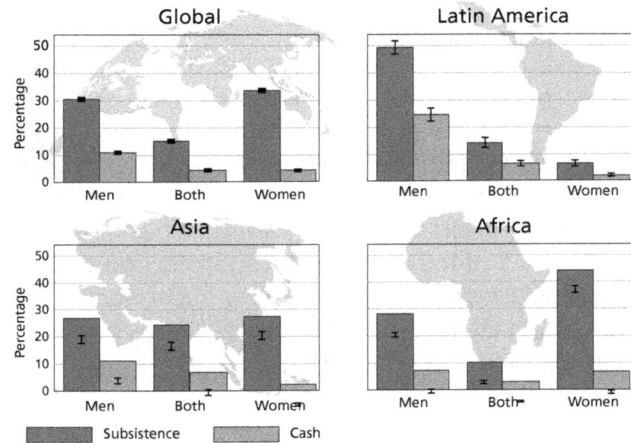

Source: Sunderland et al. (2014)

Scaling up the commercialization of NTFPs and other forest resources can lead to overexploitation and resource depletion, putting additional pressures on both women and men in forest-dependent communities in terms of the use of their time and competition for land on which to produce these resources (Dancer and Tsikata 2015, Marshall *et al.* 2006).

Unequal access to forest resources

Restricted access to forest resources by people who are dependent on these resources (especially female-led households) can result in food insecurity, low resilience to disasters and environmental change, and lower incomes. In recent decades considerable efforts have been made by national government and international development programmes to support the poor, particularly women, in gaining greater economic and decision-making empowerment, including access to and control

59

over forest resources, often through promoting and implementing community-based forest management programmes and through forest user groups (FUGs) – groups of people living in the vicinity of forests who are entrusted to manage and conserve them, develop forest resources, and utilize forest products. FUGs are actively involved in a range of community forestry processes (Forestry Nepal 2016). Participating in them can help women increase their incomes and knowledge, but barriers including social structures and cultural norms, lack of intra-household negotiation power, and household responsibilities may keep them from taking full advantage of such opportunities (Sunderland *et al.* 2014, Sunderlin *et al.* 2007).

Degradation of forest resources: increasing scale and impacts

Wildlife poaching and trade

Illegal wildlife poaching and trade continue to increase internationally at an alarming rate (Wasser 2015, Wittemeyer *et al.* 2014, Niraj 2009). They can have severe negative impacts on wild populations, including biodiversity loss, disease, and the introduction of invasive species. Traders and consumers of wildlife products are rarely defined by gender. However, treating illegal wildlife poaching and trade in a gender-blind way may prevent understanding the issues fully and finding more effective solutions, as they are highly gendered activities (Torres-Cruz and McElwee 2012).

People who take part in wildlife-related illegal activities can generally be characterized by gender as well as by social class, income level and geographical location. Men's roles in the illegal wildlife trade as both producers

(hunters) and consumers are clearer than those of women, although the latter are involved at several stages of the supply chain (e.g. as transporters or as purchasers for food and medicine processing) (Torres-Cruz and McElwee 2012). There are different demands for types of food, ornaments, medicines, decorations, and spiritual and power symbols by women and men. For example, eating wild meats and consuming other wildlife products may be believed to increase men's sexual prowess; other products are believed to be good for women's health, such as bear bile (Liu *et al.* 2016, Hance 2015).

In 2015 a South African ranger group consisting mostly of women, the Black Mamba Anti-Poaching Unit, was one of the winners of the top United Nations environmental prize. Since its inception in 2013, the 26-member unit has reduced snaring by 76%, removed more than 1000 snares, and put five poachers' camps and two bush meat kitchens out of action.

Gender and artisanal and small-scale mining

The social and economic impacts of land-based extractive industry operations include displacement of local communities including indigenous people, increased threats to food security, and loss of livelihoods in forest-dependent communities. Many of these impacts fall unequally on women and men in local communities.

There are approximately 100 million artisanal miners globally, an estimated 30% of whom are women (ranging from 10-25% in some Asian countries up to 25-50% in parts of Africa) (AU and AMCC 2015). Working at artisanal and small-scale mining (ASM) sites silica dust. Contamination by mercury used in gold recovery has significant impacts not only on women, men and children working at ASM sites, but on other people in the vicinity and those living in downstream areas (specifically young children and women who are pregnant and breastfeeding) (AU and AMCC 2015, Cordy *et al.* 2011, HRW 2010)

Land grabbing of forest land and resources

Land grabbing is a global phenomenon that has had significant economic, environmental and social impacts during the last decade or so, frequently resulting in conflict between local communities and outsiders (IIED 2016b, Dhiaulhaq 2014, Cotula and Vermeulen 2010). Land grabs are often followed by the introduction of chemically intensive, industrial-scale monoculture production such as oil palm, sugarcane, and and other crops for animal feed.

was once considered too dangerous for women, but the number of women in this sector has been increasing for a number of years. In many locations women's multiple roles include care-giving and participation in the sex trade. They are often subject to sexual abuse and health risks such as HIV/AIDS. Women's contributions to mining enterprises are often invisible because they perform unrecognized and undervalued care and domestic work. Despite heavy involvement of women in ASM, men control and own most of the family's assets, including land, the income from mining and farming, tools, homes, crops and the benefits yielded.

The dangerous conditions in which many miners work are not surprising, given the informal and often illegal nature of ASM. Women and men miners are endangered through handling and misuse of chemicals such as mercury and cyanide, accidents due to landslides or explosions, and lung diseases due to exposure to

The environmental, economic and health effects of monoculture plantations include: fragmentation (threatening forest biodiversity); loss of agrobiodiversity; serious negative effects on people in forest-dependent communities, further restricting their already limited access to forest resources and marginalizing them from their daily life activities such as water collection and traditional livelihoods; and indirect health impacts due to use of agrochemicals, as well as smoke and dust (Fonjong 2014, Hahn *et al.* 2014, De Schutter 2009). Large-scale land deals which do not take into account local gender dimensions will perpetuate existing gender inequality and may contribute to increased resource scarcity, poverty, people displacement, tension across generations due to loss of land and livelihoods, and other types of conflicts (White and Park 2015, Verma 2014, Behrman 2012).

Community-based forest management supporting gender equality

In forest-dependent communities women play a key role in forest management but are often excluded from decision-making (IIED 2012, Onta 2012, OECD 2010). Drawing on data collected from over 8000 households across research sites in Africa, Asia and Latin America, Sunderland et al. (2014) concluded that women's participation in forest user groups was far less than that of men and below their proportionate use of forests. Excluding women from decision-making can lead to ineffective forest protection and inefficient forest planning (Agarwal 2001).

Community forestry initiatives, which promote equal gender participation in forest management structures at community level, are often seen as a means of obtaining both social and environmental co-benefits. Effective participation can be defined as attending meetings and speaking up during them, but it can also be defined by the share of women in office-bearing positions. The interface between gender, participation and community forestry has impacts on pre-existing gender relations and on relative participation by women and men in community forestry decision-making processes. These include changes in the intra-household decision-making process and in allocations of land, labour and capital (Djoudi and Brockhaus 2011).

Women, where documentation is available, have actively contributed to better forest conservation outcomes through increased compliance with rules, which has improved forest protection and led to significant decreases in illegal grazing and logging

(Agarwal 2009). Although both women and men in forest-dependent communities possess traditional knowledge of use of forest ecosystems, enhancing women's roles in the biodiversity conservation and the protection of forest ecosystems is crucial, including through preservation of indigenous seeds and medicinal plants (Mulyoutami et al. 2013, Voeks 2007).

Increasing the number of women and members of other disadvantaged groups on forest management executive committees can bring about improved distributional equity, as shown in a study on community forestry groups in India and Nepal (Agarwal 2015). However, providing policy advice to promote equal participation without carefully understanding local and non-local economic, cultural and socio-political processes should be cautioned against.

A simple "win-win" relationship between gender equality and the environment cannot be assumed. Perceiving dynamics around women's exclusion as the sole power struggle within community forestry risks overlooking differences and inequalities among – or affecting – women and men based on various other socio-economic factors such as ethnicity, class, age and religion. This underscores the importance of both understanding gender as a contextual and intersectional concept and viewing women (like men) as individual agents, constrained by structures of varying flexibility, whose identities, preferences and aspirations cannot be reduced to simplistic, general and often empirically unfounded stereotypes.

Gender and REDD+

Comparing women's participation in forest management and decision-making in 18 Reducing Emissions from Deforestation and Forest Degradation (REDD+) sites in five countries, Larson *et al.* (2015) observed that women's involvement in decision-making was limited and that significantly fewer women than men had knowledge and information about REDD+. In an analysis of the Green Belt Movement in Kenya and Community Forestry Programs in Nepal, Boyer-Rechlin (2010) highlighted the importance of taking account of pre-existing gender roles and cultural contexts, as well as investing in civic education and building women's skills.

Among the many factors that influence successful implementation of a REDD+ scheme (e.g. baseline CO_2 emissions, records of forest carbon stock, condition of biodiversity, quality of governance), it is important that safeguards are in place to secure land rights and full participation by local communities in order to achieve "win-win" effects on both poverty alleviation and environmental protection (Mahanty and McDermott 2013, Lawlor *et al.* 2013). The UN-REDD programme developed guidance to promote gender-sensitive processes in the preparation, implementation and monitoring of REDD+ projects and other action plans which focus on strengthening a bottom-up approach, including priority alignment to national needs and capacities (FAO/UNDP/UNEP 2013). However, mainstreaming gender in national policies, in which is often interpreted as an increased number of women participating at local level, is not sufficient to realize the full potential of women and men as agents of change at community level. Several reports have

suggested that gender should be carefully integrated in the design, monitoring and evaluation of REDD+ programmes, including gender-sensitive indicators and safeguard approaches. Systematic gender-responsive analysis should be carried out, including information on decision-making, gender perceptions and actual gender differences in interests in, as well as needs for effective engagement of women and men in REDD+ implementation in local contexts (Eggerts 2016, Larson *et al.* 2015, Gurung and Setyowati 2012).

References

Agarwal, B. (2015). The power of numbers in gender dynamics: illustrations from community forestry groups, *The Journal of Peasant Studies,* 42(1), 1-20.

Agarwal, B. (2010). Does Women's Proportional Strength Affect their Participation? Governing Local Forests in South Asia, *World Development,* 38(1), 98-112

Agarwal, B. (2009). Rule making in community forestry institutions: The difference women make, *Ecological Economics,* 68(8-9), 2296-2308.

Agarwal, B. (2001). Participatory Exclusions, Community Forestry, and Gender: An Analysis for South Asia and a Conceptual Framework, *World Development,* 29 (10), 1623-1648.

Aguilar, L., Quesada-Aguilar, A. and Shaw, D.M.P. (2011). *Forests and Gender,* International Union for Conservation of Nature (IUCN), Women's Environment and Development Organization (WEDO), Gland, Switzerland and New York.

AU and AMCC (2015). *African Women in Artisinal and Small-Scale Mining.* African Union and African Mineral Development Centre.

Azzez, F.A., Obafunso, E.O, Jaiyesimi, M.A., Akanbi F.S. and Nosiru S.M.O (2014). Women's Involvement in the utilization of non-timber forest products. Society for Advancement of Sciences. *Journal of Biological and Chemical Research*, 31(1), 73-80.

Behrman, J., Meinzen-Dick, R., and Quisumbing, A. (2012). The gender implications of large-scale land deals. The Journal of Peasant Studies, 39(1), 49-79.

Boyer-Rechlin, B. (2010). Women in forestry: A study of Kenya's Green Belt Movement and Nepal's Community Forestry Program, *Scandinavian Journal of Forest Research,* 25 (sup 9), 69-72.

Chao, S. (2012). *Forest Peoples: Numbers across the world.* Forest Peoples Programme, Moreton-in-Marsh, UK.

Cordy, P., Veiga, M.M., Salih, I., Al-Saadi, S., Console, S., Garcia, O., Mesa, L.A., Velásquez-López, P.C. and Roeser, M. (2011). Mercury contamination from artisanal gold mining in Antioguia, Colombia: The world's highest per capita mercury pollution, *Science of the Total Environment,* 410-11, 154-60.

Cotula, L. and Vermeulen, S. (2010). Over the Heads of Local People: Consultation, Consent and Recompense in Large-Scale Land Deals for Biofuels Projects in Africa. *Journal of Peasant Studies*, 37, 4, 899-916.

Dancer, H.and Tsikata, D. (2015). *Commercial Agriculture in Sub-Sahara Agriculture with a Gender Perspective: Concepts, Issues and Methods,* Land and Agricultural Commercialisation in Africa (LACA) Working Paper 132, Future Agricultures Consortium Secretariat, University of Sussex, Brighton.

De Schutter, O. (2009). Large-scale land acquisitions and leases: A set of core principles and measures to address the human rights challenge. UN.

Dhiaulhaq, A., Gritten, D., De Bruyn, T., Yasmi, Y., Zazali, A., and Silalahi, M. (2014). Transforming conflict in plantations through mediation: Lessons and experiences from Sumatera, Indonesia. Forest Policy and Economics, 41(0).

Djoudi, H. and Brockhaus, M. (2011). *Is adaptation to climate change gender neutral?: Lessons from communities dependent on livestock and forests in northern Mali.* Center for International Forestry Research (CIFOR), Bogor.

EC (2007). *Attitudes on issues related to EU Energy Policy; Analytical Report.* The Gallup Organization Flash Eurobarometer 206. Brussels, Belgium: European Commission

Eggerts, E. (2016) The Path through the woods: Gender-responsive REDD+ policy and action. In L. Aguilar, M. Granat, and C. Owren (Authors), *Roots for the future: The landscape and way forward on gender and climate change.* IUCN and GGCA, Washington, DC.

FAO (n.d.). Numbers of Forest "Dependent" People and Types of Forest Relationships, FAO, Rome.

FAO/UNDP/UNEP (2013). G*uidance Note on Gender Sensitive REDD+*. UN-REDD, Geneva.

Fonjong, L. N. and Fokum, V. Y. (2015). Rethinking the water dimension of large scale land acquisitions in sub-Saharan Africa. Journal of African Studies and Development, 7(4), 112 - 120

Forestry Nepal (2016). Forest User Groups [Website]. http://www.forestrynepal.org/wiki/138.

Hance, J. (2015). Is the end of "house of horror" bear bile factories in sight? [Online]. Guardian (London), 9 April 2015. Available at: http://www.theguardian.com/environment/radical-conservation/2015/apr/09/bear-bile-china-synthetic-alternative

Hahn, M.B., Gagnon, R.E., Barcellos, C., Asner, G.P., Patz and J.A. (2014). Influence of Deforestation, Logging, and Fire on Malaria in the Brazilian Amazon, PLoS ONE 9(1): e85725

HRW (2010). *Mercury: A Health and Human Rights Issue.* Human Rights Watch.

IIED (2016). Understanding growing pressures on land: 'Land grabbing' and beyond. [Online]: http://www.iied.org/understanding-growing-pressures-land-land-grabbing-beyond. IIED, London.

IIED (2012). His REDD+, her REDD+: how integrating gender can improve readiness, IIED, London.

Larson, A.M., Dokken, T., Duchelle, A.E., Atmadja, S., I.A.P., R., Cronkleton, P., Cromberg, M., Sunderlin, W.D., Awono, A. and Selaya, G. (2015). *The role of women in early REDD+ implementation: lessons for future engagement,* CIFOR, Bogor.

Lawlor, K., Madeira, E., Blockhus, J. and Ganz, D. (2013). Community Participation and Benefits in REDD+: A Review of Initial Outcomes and Lessons, *Forests,* 4(2), 296-318.

Liu, Z., Jiang, Z., Fang, H., Li. C., Mi, A., Chen, J., Zhang, X., Cui, S., Chen, D., Ping, X., Li, F., Li, C., Tang, S., Luo. Z., Zeng, Y., Meng, Z (2016). Perception, Price and Preference: Consumption and Protection of Wild Animals Used in Traditional Medicine, *PLoS One,* 1, 11(3).

Mahanty, S. and McDermott, C. (2013). How does 'Free, Prior and Informed Consent'(FPIC) impact social equity? Lessons from mining and forestry and their implications for REDD+, *Land Use Policy,* vol. 35, 406-416.

Marshall, E., Schreckenberg, K., Newton, A.C. (eds.) (2006). *Commercialization of Non-timber Forest Products: Factors Influencing Success. Lessons Learned from Mexico and Bolivia and Policy Implications for Decision-makers.* UNEP and World Conservation Monitoring Centre (WCMC).

Mulyoutami, E., Martini, E., Khususiyah, N., Suyanto, I. (2013). Gender, livelihood and land in South and Southeast Sulawesi. ICRAF Working paper No. 158. International Council for Research in Agroforestry (ICRAF), Bogor.

Niraj, S.K. (2009). Sustainable development, poaching, and illegal wildlife trade in India. Dissertation, University of Arizona.

OECD (2010). *The Governance Cluster. Climate change and gender: economic empowerment of women through climate mitigation and adaptation?*, OECD, Paris.

Onta, N. (2012). When pigs fly: why is including women in managing forests still so unusual? [Blog], International Institute for Environment and Development, London.

Sunderland, T., Achdiawan, R., Angelsen, A., Babigumira, R., Ickowitz, A., Paumgarten, F., Reyes-García, V. and Shively, G. (2014). Challenging Perceptions about Men, Women, and Forest Product Use: A Global Comparative Study, *World Development,* 64 (Sup 1), S56-S66.

Sunderlin, W.D., Dewi, S. and Puntodewo, A. (2007). Poverty and forests: multi-country analysis of spatial association and proposed policy solutions, *CIFOR Occasional Paper* No. 47, Bogor, Indonesia.

Torres-Cruz, M.L. and McElwee, P. (2012). *Gender and Sustainability: Lessons from Asia and Latin America.* University of Arizona Press, Tuscon.

UN (2014). *The World Survey on the role of women in development 2014: Gender equality and sustainable development,* UN Women.

Verma, R. (2014). Land Grabs, Powers, and Gender in East and Southern Africa: So, What's New? *Feminist Economics,* 20(1), 52-75.

Voeks, R.A. (2007). Are women reservoirs of traditional plant knowledge? Gender, ethnobotany and globalization in northeast Brazil, *Singapore Journal of Tropical Geography,* 28(1), 7-20.

Wasser, S. (2015). How forensic intelligence helps combat illegal wildlife trade. World Bank, *Voices: Perspectives on Development.*

White, B. and Park, C. M. (2015). Gender and generation in Southeast Asia's corporate 'rush to land': a brief introduction. Paper presentation. Conference: *Land grabbing, conflict and agrarian-environmental transformation: perspective from East and Southeast Asia,* 5-6 June 2015, Chiang Mai.

Wittemeyer, G., Northrup, J.M., Douglas-Hamilton, I., Omundi, P. and Burnham, K.P. (2014). Illegal killing for ivory drives global decline in African elephants. *Proceedings of the National Academy of Sciences of the United States of America,* 11 (36), 13117-13121.

Wunder, S., Börner, J., Shively, G. and Wyman, M. (2014). Safety Nets, Gap Filling and Forests: A Global-Comparative Perspective, *World Development.* 64, Supp 1 Forests, Livelihoods, and Conservation, S29-S42.

WWF (2012). *Forest Management and Gender.* WWF.

This report reviews a number of sectors, topics and issues in relation to the linkages between gender and environment. All of them share some common factors that influence the analysis, including disasters, climate change, conflicts and health. These have been identified as "cross-cutting issues" for the sections in Chapter 2. They have close connections to human and environmental vulnerability, and many of these connections have been discussed in the previous sections of this chapter. This section briefly examines the complex intersections between these issues, with a focus on gender and the environment – which is often seen as a cross-cutting issue itself.

2.7

Disasters

For many years disasters were defined by a "hazards" approach in which physical parameters were prioritized over socio-political variables in understanding causation, response, mitigation and recovery. Disasters were often represented as large-scale, rare and extreme environmental events. However, hazards exist and disasters occur in the context of everyday realities defined by natural resource management, poverty, and social inequalities of many kinds (Blaikie *et al.* 2014, Hewitt 2014, O'Keefe *et al.* 1976).

The gender-differentiated evidence base in this field is growing, demonstrating the always-gendered nature of disasters at any point in the disaster cycle and whatever the hazard types. Neumayer and Plümper (2007) have argued convincingly through statistical analysis that the socially constructed, gender-specific vulnerabilities of females within everyday socio-economic patterns lead to higher female disaster mortality rates. More females die (and at a younger age) than males, but this is tied closely to their socio-economic standing. The adverse impacts of disasters on females relative to males decrease as the socio-economic status of females rises. This is a powerful argument in favour of an intersectional gendered analysis rather than a simple biological sex-based investigation.

Specific disaster cases require an open approach. For example, in the 2004 Indian Ocean tsunami after which, according to Oxfam (2005), male survivors in Indonesia outnumbered female survivors by a ratio of almost 3:1, in the worst case 80% of deaths were female. The Oxfam report is supported by Rofi *et al.* (2006), who found that two-thirds of tsunami deaths

in Aceh Province, Indonesia, were female. A high percentage of female fatalities is common but not universal. In a few disasters data show more male deaths: in the 1995 Chicago heat wave in the United States, elderly African American men were more likely to die (Kleinenberg 2002); in other cases, especially in floods, young males seem particularly vulnerable through a greater propensity for risk-taking behavior (Jonkman and Kelman 2005).

Women are often disadvantaged in many other ways in environmental disasters. They are under-represented in both formal and informal decision-making roles, pre- and post-disaster (Fordham 2003). Although women are more likely to believe warnings and have a greater propensity to act upon them, gendered power relations mean that men often make the decisions (Tyler and Fairbrother 2013). Women from lower-income and more socially marginalized groups experience higher rates of gender-based violence (GBV) during disasters, although the relatively recent upsurge of research into GBV in disasters suggests it is prevalent across social and class divides (Ajibade *et al.* 2013, Enarson 2012).

There is a small but growing evidence base focused on the lived experiences of gender and sexual minority groups during environmental disasters. In the Asia-Pacific region, for example, there are many recognized cross-gender groups such as the *whakawahine* in New Zealand, the *fa'afafine* in Samoa, and the *bakla* in the Philippines (Gaillard *et al.* 2015, Gaillard 2011, Pincha 2008). Research has identified the specific vulnerability and marginalization, and also the capacities and contributions, of the bakla during the 2009 cyclones in Quezon City (Gaillard *et al.* 2015, Gaillard 2011). They were given "dirty" jobs and fed last in their

Bangkok flooding in 2011.
Photo credit: © Ruchos/ shutterstock.com

households, but were also recognized more positively for their community disaster response activities. Despite this emerging understanding, the consideration of gender, in both policy and practice, is generally couched in "heteronormative" terms as a binary sex variable: female or male. Rarely are categories of sexual orientation or alternative identities included, despite considerable advocacy by lesbian, gay, bisexual and transgender (LGBT) communities of interest and even cautioning statements by the UN Secretary-General Ban Ki-moon, who describes homophobic discrimination as "one of the great, neglected human rights challenges of our time" (UN 2013).

Climate change

Climate change impacts, policy and other related factors are similarly gender-differentiated but are less well documented, partly because of the uncertainty

of attributing any single event to climate change and also because this category has been dominated, longer than the disaster category, by a physical sciences approach in which social scientific approaches have struggled to achieve acceptance. However, climate change adaptation and disaster risk reduction (DRR) are clearly interlinked, as evidenced by the fact that 91% of recorded major disasters caused by natural hazards from 1994 to 2013 were climate and weather events (IUCN 2015, UNISDR n.d.).

Climate change, understood as an identifiable change in the state of the climate (from whatever cause) that lasts for an extended period (IPCC 2012), provides a backdrop of uncertainty for all the topics addressed in the GGEO report. The projected increase in extreme weather and climate events unsettles the (admittedly often tenuous) statistical likelihood of repeated events such as floods or storms and makes planning, mitigation or adaptation a challenge for individuals, communities and countries.

All evidence on migrations shows they are highly gendered, whether migration is caused by environmental change or poor governance and whether it is voluntary, compelled or involuntary (O'Hagan 2015, Fröhlich and Gioli 2015, Detraz and Windsor 2014, Wodon et al. 2014, World Bank 2014). Women and men migrate in almost equal numbers overall, but their triggers to move and subsequent experiences are different and contingent. People already in a vulnerable position are likely to be hardest hit by disasters and compelled migration, and to be at higher risk overall of climate-generated violence and conflict of various kinds.

Migration is a coping or adaptation strategy to deal with extremes of environmental change. Projected changes in climate will lead to changes in the frequency, intensity, spatial extent, duration and extremes of weather and climate events (IPCC 2012). In a link to our analyzed sectors and other cross-cutting domains of interest, such changes will almost certainly have direct impacts on people's food security, water and sanitation, livelihoods and lifestyle, and health through the increased frequency or extremes of heat waves, flooding, droughts and rising sea levels, and indirectly through health impacts such as expansion (spatially and temporally) of infectious diseases, mental health impacts, or disruption to food supply. All of these are associated with mental health impacts such as stress, anxiety and depression (Climate and Development Knowledge Network 2012, IPCC 2012). Thus climate change is intricately linked with health and other development concerns; it will increase risks for geographically exposed locations and for the most vulnerable groups in society, often but not always including women.

A range of adaptation options could bring multiple benefits and not just costs. Suitably gender-responsive early warning systems of various kinds can provide necessary alerts to trigger a pre-emptive rather than reactive response. Enhancing food security can bring many benefits, not least to women and girls who tend to eat least and last in many parts of the world. Investing in public health infrastructure, education interventions, and processes to reduce infectious disease incidence (among many other examples) could improve the everyday situation of millions across the world.

While global warming may be inevitable, the projected extreme negative impacts (especially for marginalized groups) are not. They are contingent upon how the global "community'" of UN Member States and local communities approach the mitigation and adaptation challenge.

Conflicts

The assumption and imposition of different gendered roles and responsibilities that prevail in peacetime continue during times of conflict, often in more extreme forms. In post-conflict reconstruction, as well as in conflict analysis, the international community typically frames women and men in strict and stereotypical gender roles that further reinforce inequalities in post-conflict situations (Puechguirbal 2012).

Women are sidelined in peace talks and negotiations because of a strict division of labour that reassigns traditional roles and responsibilities to women and men in the reconstruction process; women are characterized as vulnerable victims, inextricably linked with children, irrespective of the way war and conflict force untraditional responsibilities on them as they lead in the absence of men.

To the extent that war and conflict are conventionally perceived as gendered, it is often assumed that the major impacts are on male combatants. However, while this may be the case according to a narrow reading of militarized conflicts, a broader view of the whole conflict period reveals that in many ways women are more adversely affected than men (Plumper and Neumayer 2006). Mirroring the findings for disasters more generally, it is in locations where women face daily discrimination in peacetime that they are also most severely impacted in times of conflict (Enloe 2016, Plumper and Neumayer 2006). Factors contributing to adverse life outcomes for women in times of conflict include:

- exposure to dangers arising from the difficulties of securing water, food and fuel, over and above normal family care;

- poor health outcomes as a result of damage to (collateral) health infrastructure and disruption of health services;

- increased risk of infectious and sexually transmitted diseases from conflict-generated displacement;

- economic impacts arising from rising prices and scarcities which make it difficult to meet basic needs;

- targeted violence against women through trafficking, sexual slavery and systematic rape as a weapon of war;

Natural resources underpin livelihoods for the vast majority of populations worldwide. They are often fundamental to economic recovery and development in conflict-affected settings. Exclusions or restrictions imposed on access to natural resources by certain communities and groups of people are examples of the structural inequalities and discrimination that can ultimately destabilize a peaceful society. This is most evident in regard to land tenure, but extends to access and usage rights to renewable resources such as water, as well as equitable distribution of benefits from extractive resources including minerals, metals, timber and oil. Addressing issues of inequality related to natural resource access, participation and decision-making is a critical condition for lasting peace and development.

Health

Women and men have different roles and responsibilities that shape their interactions with, risks from, and control over their environment. Their biological and physiological differentiation creates gender-differentiated risks for reproductive health in particular. For example, pregnant women are particularly susceptible to malaria-carrying mosquitoes; this puts them at particular risk in the context of the rise in global temperatures expected as a result of climate change, which is also expected to lead to shifts in water-borne and vector-borne diseases (WHO 2012).

Actual risks to women and to men will vary according to local traditions of gendered divisions of labour in which women might be more at risk from indoor pollutants, or pollutants related to traditional female employment patterns such as the export flower industry, or to supplying resources for the household (water, food, forest products); men might be more at risk in regard to occupations such as working in mines or as open-ocean fishers (WHO 2016, Levine et al. 2001). This simplified picture does not take account of women's and men's socio-economic status, land tenure/land rights, and many other factors.

The complex webs of the social determinants of health relative to those that are biologically determined tend to be underexplored. A recent example of such complex webs is the Zika virus which has emerged as a major public health risk **(Box 7).**

Box 7: The Zika virus: a convergence of unsustainable development, gender politics and ecological disruption

The emergence of the Zika virus (ZIKV) as a public health threat in the Americas in 2015, and the initial policy responses to it in early 2016, offer a case study that brings into sharp focus the importance of gender-informed environmental policies – and, conversely, the ineffectiveness of developing environmental policies in a gender vacuum. The initial policy responses to the emergence of ZIKV framed the problem primarily through a biological lens without incorporating a gender perspective, exemplifying the pervasive gap between social and environmental policy.

The ecology: ZIKV is a Flavivirus transmitted to humans by bites from arthropods, particularly the *Aedes* mosquito. Other Flaviviruses include dengue fever and yellow fever. The precise combination of factors that brought ZIKV to the Americas is not yet known. Like many insect-borne emerging diseases, it is the consequence of complex interactions between ecological disruption, climate change and human behaviour (Centers for Disease Control and Prevention 2016).

Confusing gender analysis with sex analysis: In humans, ZIKV can cause several neurological impairments including Guillain-Barré syndrome. ZIKV appears to be able to cross the placental barrier, which means that a foetus may be susceptible to the virus if infected mosquitos bite a pregnant woman. Microcephaly in newborns is strongly associated with ZIKV infection. As the arrival of ZIKV in the Americas became evident, and given concerns about the threats to foetuses, public health attention in Latin America turned quickly to women. One of the first responses by government authorities in several countries in the region, including Colombia, Ecuador, El Salvador, Honduras and Jamaica, was simply to advise women to "not to get pregnant" for various periods between six months and two years until the possible link between ZIKV and microcephaly was further established.

Such policy approaches confuse sex analysis with gender analysis, positioning women primarily as biological vessels. As policy nostrums these suggestions represent a striking disregard for the realities under which women become pregnant, the extent to which they may not control their own reproductive lives, or the extent to which they have sexual autonomy. Globally about 40% of all pregnancies are unintended; in Latin America and the Caribbean this figure is 56% (Sedgh *et al.* 2014). It is evident that women are not fully or solely responsible for determining whether or not they "get pregnant."

A policy focus that makes men's role in creating pregnancies invisible is guaranteed to fail. Further, the "avoid pregnancy" suggestions by health ministers cruelly disregard the reality that many of the same governments restrict abortion rights and contraceptives distribution, thus further denying women the power to manage their own reproductive lives.

In terms of vulnerability to ZIKV, social inequality intersects with gender dynamics: people living in the poorest urban communities lacking municipal services (and with uncontrolled waste and standing water) are at particularly high risk of mosquito exposure (Diniz 2016). Women who live in substandard housing are more likely to become ZIKV infected in the first place, and then to be the least likely to be able to protect themselves (or a foetus they are carrying) from the health effects.

Contd...

Precaution and pesticides

In 1962, in *Silent Spring*, the scientist Rachel Carson revealed the high environmental costs of indiscriminate use of pesticides. Yet decades after *Silent Spring*, health authorities across Latin America responded to the ZIKV threat by immediately resorting to aggressive campaigns of saturation spraying of pesticides – in interior spaces, along roadways, around waterways and throughout urban neighbourhoods. While there is vigorous debate in the public health field on the benefits and drawbacks of insecticide use (and evidence of strong disease-control benefits from targeted uses of specific pesticides), ecological harm and problems with insecticide resistance are inevitable byproducts of wide-scale pesticide campaigns. Environmental precautionary principles suggest that in the face of uncertainty, actions – particularly those taken in haste – need to be weighed in terms of possible (irrevocable) harm. However, in this case the initial policy responses showed little of the restraint and considered judgment that during the past 50 years of ecological and gender analysis have been shown to be appropriate.

References

Aguilar, L., Granat, M., and Owren, C. (2015). *Roots for the future: The landscape and way forward on gender and climate. Washington, DC:* IUCN and GGCA.

Ajibade, I., McBean, G. and Bezner-Kerr, R. (2013). Urban flooding in Lagos, Nigeria: Patterns of vulnerability and resilience among women, *Global Environmental Change,* 23(6), 1714-1725.

Blaikie, P., Cannon, T., Davis, I. and Wisner, B. (2014). *At risk: natural hazards, people's vulnerability and disasters.* Routledge, London.

Carson, R. (1962). *Silent Spring.* Houghton Mifflin, NY.

Centers for Disease Control and Prevention (2016). Areas with Zika. http://www.cdc.gov/zika/geo/.

Climate and Development Knowledge Network (2012). *Managing Climate Extremes and Disasters in the Health Sector: Lessons from the IPCC SREX Report* Climate and Development Knowledge Network.

Detraz, N. and Windsor, L. (2014). Evaluating Climate Migration: Population Movement, Insecurity and Gender, *International Feminist Journal of Politics,* 16(1), 127-146.

Diniz, D. (2016). The Zika Virus and Brazilian Women's Right to Choose, *The New York Times,* FEB 8 2016. [Online] Available at: http://www.nytimes.com/2016/02/08/opinion/the-zika-virus-and-brazilian-womens-right-to-choose.html?_r=0

Enarson, E.P. (2012). *Women confronting natural disaster*: From vulnerability to resilience. Lynne Rienner Publishers Boulder, Colorado.

Enloe, C. 2016. *Globalization and Militarism: Feminists Make the Link.* Rowman and Littlefield, Maryland USA.

Fordham, M. (2003). Gender, disaster and development: the necessity of integration. In *Natural Disaster and Development in a Globalizing World.* (Ed). M. Pelling. Routledge, London, 57-74.

Fröhlich, C. and Gioli, G. (2015). Gender, Conflict, and Global Environmental Change, Peace Review, 27(2), 137-146.

Gaillard, J., Sanz, K. and Fordham, M. (2015). Culture, Gender and Sexuality: Perspectives for Disaster Risk Reduction. In *Cultures and Disasters: Understanding Cultural Framings in Disaster Risk Reduction.* Eds. Fred Krüger, Greg Bankoff, Terry Cannon, Benedikt Orlowski and E.L.F. Schipper. Routledge, London.

Gaillard, J.C. (2011). People's Response to Disasters: Vulnerability, Capacities and Resilience in Philippine Context. Center for Kapampangan Studies, Angeles City, Pampanga, Philippines.

Hewitt, K. (2014). *Regions of Risk: A Geographical Introduction to Disasters.* Routledge, London.

IPCC (2012). *Managing the Risks of Extreme Events and Disasters to Advance Climate Change Adaptation. A Special Report of Working Groups I and II of the Intergovernmental Panel on Climate Change* IPCC, Cambridge, New York.

Jonkman, S. N., and Kelman, I. (2005). An analysis of the causes and circumstances of flood disaster deaths. *Disasters,* 29(1), 75-97.

Klinenberg, E. (2002). *Heat Wave: A Social Autopsy of Disaster in Chicago.* University of Chicago Press.

Levine, J.A., Weisell, R., Chevassus, S., Martinez, C.D., Burlingame, B. and Coward, W.A. (2001). The work burden of women, *Science,* 294 (5543), pp. 812-812.

Neumayer, E. and Plümper, T. (2007). The gendered nature of natural disasters: the impact of catastrophic events on the gender gap in life expectancy, 1981–2002. *Annals of the Association of American Geographers,* 97 (3). 551-566.

O'Hagan, E.M. (2015). Mass migration is no 'crisis': it's the new normal as the climate changes, *The Guardian,* 18 Aug 2015. [Online] Available at: http://www.theguardian.com/commentisfree/2015/aug/18/mass-migration-crisis-refugees-climate-change.

O'Keefe, P., Westgate, K. and Wisner, B. (1976). Taking the naturalness out of natural disasters, *Nature,* 260, 566-567.

Oxfam (2005). The tsunami's impact on women [Online]. Available at: http://www.oxfam.org/en/policy/bn050326-tsunami-women

Pincha, C. (2008). *Gender Sensitive Disaster Management: A Toolkit for Practioners.* (81-86945-20-2), Earthworm Books, Mumbai.

Plumper, T. and Neumayer, E. (2006). The unequal burden of war: The effect of armed conflict on the gender gap in life expectancy, *International organization,* 60(3), 723.

Puechguirbal N. (2012). The Cost of Ignoring Gender in Conflict and Post-Conflict Situations: A Feminist Perspective, *Amsterdam Law Forum* Vol 4:1 4-19.

Rofi, A., Doocy, S. and Robinson, C. (2006). Tsunami mortality and displacement in Aceh province, Indonesia, *Disasters,* 30(3), 340-350.

Sedgh, G., Singh, S. and Hussain, R. (2014). Intended and Unintended Pregnancies Worldwide in 2012 and Recent Trends. *Studies in Family Planning,* 45: 301–314.

Tyler, M. and Fairbrother, P. (2013). Bushfires are "men's business": The importance of gender and rural hegemonic masculinity, *Journal of Rural Studies,* 30, 110-119.

UN (2013). Secretary-General's video message to the Oslo Conference on Human Rights, Sexual Orientation and Gender Identity [Online]. Available at: http://www.un.org/sg/STATEMENTS/index.asp?nid=6736.

UNISDR (n.d.) Climate Change Adaptation [Website]. Available at: http://www.unisdr.org/we/advocate/climate-change.

Prüss-Ustün, A., Wolf, J., Corvalán, C., Bos, R. and Neira, M. (2016). *Preventing disease through healthy environments: a global assessment of the burden of disease from environmental risks.* WHO, Geneva.

Wodon, Q., Liverani, A., Joseph, G., Bougnoux, N. (2014). *Climate change and migration : evidence from the Middle East and North Africa.* World Bank Group, Washington DC.

OUTLOOK FOR A SUSTAINABLE AND JUST FUTURE - FROM BUSINESS-AS-USUAL APPROACHES TOWARDS TRANSFORMATIONAL CHANGE

"Human beings are at the centre of concerns for sustainable development. They are entitled to a healthy and productive life in harmony with nature."
Principles 1 and 20, Rio Declaration on Environment and Development

Photo Credit: © Le Bich

CHAPTER

3

Key Messages

Gender and environment approaches are necessary for sustainable, equitable and just management of the planet's natural resources and ecosystems.

- Business-as-usual approaches are not working. Instead, they are proving disastrous for people and the planet alike. Gender-and-environment approaches are integral to a sustainable and just future.
- Until recently, gender and the environment were treated in separate silos.
- While the gender-and-environment nexus is increasingly acknowledged in international agreements and national policy documents, implementation and follow-through are weak or absent.
- Gender equality cannot be measured by women's and men's "presence" alone. Presence does not necessarily mean "participation", and neither inherently implies "influence": the nature of people's participation is what makes their presence meaningful.
- A transformative agenda recognizes gender equality as a driver of social change, leading to more people-smart environmental policies.

The 2030 Agenda for Sustainable Development places women's rights at the centre of transformative change, and especially at the centre of the pursuit of sustainable development in its three dimensions – economic, social and environmental (UN 2015). Giving shape and context to what gender-transformative sustainable development approaches look like, it offers the promise of shifting current trends and dynamics away from business as usual (BAU) in regard to gender and the environment. However, even in a document as visionary as the 2030 Agenda, explicit links between gender and the environment are weak: in the environmentally specific SDG goals, gender and women are mentioned in only one target: "13.b, Promote mechanisms for raising capacity for effective climate change-related planning and management in least developed countries and small island developing States, including focusing on women, youth and local and marginalized communities."

While the gender-and-environment nexus is increasingly acknowledged in international agreements and national policy documents, implementation and follow-through need to be strengthened. The extent and gravity of global environmental crises call for a decisive move away from business-as-usual.

Environmental decisions and decision-makers are gendered. Systems of political power and economic systems are shaped by cultural norms in which gender presumptions are embedded. Environmental decisions and outcomes cannot be mapped directly onto gender decisions and outcomes, and while greater gender equality would not magically solve all environmental problems (and environmental sustainability would not automatically ensure greater gender equity), there are strong ideological synergies between forces of equity – or inequity – in both realms.

The future we want

The Future We Want (UN 2012) is defined by a framework for action anchored in rights, responsibilities, accountability and opportunities. Such a basis would help to achieve and sustain a world where gender equality and environmental quality are central to conceptualizing, analysing and resolving current development challenges. It would be shaped through:

- bridging the divide between the social and environmental, which starts by bringing gender analysis into environmental policies and practices;

- exposing and rejecting sectoral "silos": promoting solutions that are multi-focused, and prioritizing actions that are likely to have positive effects on gender equality, the environment and sustainable development;

- ensuring that policies that address environmental sustainability, gender equality and sustainable development will "not leave anybody behind" – a critical SDG goal;

- addressing structural violence, including gender-based violence, in current patterns of environmental degradation;

- recognizing that broad issues of identity go beyond the simple binary of "women and men" to include multiple forms of masculinity and femininity, as well as other genders;

- moving beyond a focus on numbers (or quantities) as signifying representation to methods of measuring representation that give equal attention to both quality and quantity;

- recognizing that the Rio Principles on Environment and Development (the Rio Principles) (UN 1992), particularly the principles of "common but differentiated responsibilities" and "prior informed (and informed) consent" apply both to environmental relations and to gender relations.

Embracing these principles will require a thorough understanding of the environment, of social and political realities, and of the interactions between them. It will also require a willingness to critically examine conventional environmental – and social – structures and analyses and to move beyond "business as usual" approaches in cultural as well as environmental realms.

Signs of progress in moving beyond business-as-usual and towards the future we want

Even given these large-scale impediments, there are strong signs of forward movement that point towards the future we want. These include:

Recognition that a healthy environment is a right: Accepting that a healthy environment is a "right" represents a significant step towards a healthier future. The first formal recognition of the right to a healthy environment was in the 1972 Stockholm Declaration, which emerged from the pioneering global United Nations Conference on the Human Environment. Since 1972, a rights approach to environmental concerns has increasingly been integrated in international and national policies and governance. The principle that citizens have legally enforceable rights to a healthy environment is slowly gaining currency. In many countries indigenous peoples and women's groups are at the forefront of rights-based environmental activism.

Recognition that gender equality works for all: In many ways "environmental rights" movements draw on, and have expanded in parallel with, women's rights movements. It is becoming increasingly clear that inclusiveness enhances effectiveness in all spheres of society, from the micro to the macro, and there is strong evidence that reducing gender gaps accelerates progress towards other development goals including environmental goals. Gender equality produces better health outcomes in families. Repeated analyses have demonstrated a strong positive correlation between higher GDP and greater gender equality (World Economic Forum 2015, OECD 2014). Men who live in more gender-equal societies have a better quality of life than men in less gender-equal ones (Holter 2014). Gender equality in formal governance systems brings positive environmental outcomes: evidence suggests that countries with higher parliamentary representation of women are more likely to ratify environmental agreements and more likely to set aside protected land areas (UNDP 2014).

Incorporating gender into environmental policies: Since the UN Conference on Environment and Development (UNCED) in 1992 in Rio de Janeiro, Brazil, gender aspects have received more attention in several international environmental policies. With assiduous advocacy, analytical and political work by women's groups, gender has obtained a firm purchase in several platforms, such as the UN Convention on Biological Diversity (CBD), the UN Convention to Combat Desertification (UNCCD) and the UN Framework Convention on Climate Change (UNFCCC).

Recognizing the value of citizen science: In recent years several tools have been developed to engage citizens – women and men – in knowledge building and public decision-making mechanisms. Citizen science, as mentioned in the World Economic Forum's *Global Risks Report 2016*, "is increasingly seen as a tool that could enable a more participatory democracy by empowering individuals and communities to analyse, understand and ultimately take ownership of the issues that affect them, enabling them to propose concrete and actionable solutions to decision-makers" (World Economic Forum 2016).

Revaluing traditional knowledge: The value of indigenous knowledge systems and practices is being given more recognition in international environmental fora. The traditional knowledge held by women and men – often different, but complementary – is of paramount importance for environmental conservation and sustainable development.

Gender-responsive green economies: The global call to restructure current linear and unsustainable economic dynamics (e.g. through promotion of circular economic systems green economics, and local food co-operatives of producers and users) is clear. The concept of access to (the use of) goods instead of ownership could offer interesting opportunities for both women and men, but particularly women who have been traditionally excluded from many formal asset ownership systems.

Large-scale structural forces that hold back transformational change

Large-scale structural forces, many existing for decades (and some for centuries), hinder transformative change. They include:

Conventional framing of "the environment": Environmental assessments conceptualize "the environment" in a physical, biosystem frame. The notion that the environment is socially constructed and perceived is still marginalized in much mainstream scientific environmental work. The physical-sciences-first approach sidelines social and gender analysis.

Gender disproportion in formal political domains: The formal political arena is where policies are developed and choices are made that directly shape citizens' livelihoods and well-being, including social and environmental relationships. As of April 2016, women held 50% or more of elected legislative seats in only two countries in the world, Bolivia and Rwanda; the world average was around 23% (Inter-Parliamentary Union 2016). Increasing women's representation within formal political systems is not an automatic panacea for social justice, gender equity or environmental justice. Nevertheless, the diminished presence of women in formal political institutions is emblematic of the extent to which the brain trust of half the world's population is mostly excluded from contributing to formal decision-making.

Perverse economic systems: Ecological and social systems are trapped in a vicious spiral of unsustainable economic priorities, enabled by unrealistic economic assumptions and supported by inadequate analytical tools that are bringing about environmental devastation while undermining gender equality. Environmental and gender security will be elusive as long as economic systems based on the unsustainable assumption that production and consumption can (and should) continuously grow have primacy. The same economic assumptions provide only the narrowest view of the activities and processes that propel real growth and well-being. Community activism, caring work that is not goods-based, and ecological restoration activities are the real forces that sustain economic and environmental well-being, yet none of these has a secure place in mainstream economic processes and measurements.

Pervasive gender inequality: One of the most powerful universal contexts of the current state of social and environmental relations is gender inequality. It is pervasive and universal, and is sustained by visible and invisible practices in public and private domains. Gender equality, similarly, exists on multiple planes simultaneously and progress across those planes is not even. Gender inequalities are intersectional and are magnified by other social positions. Multiple and multiplying layers of inequality are experienced by women who are indigenous; or members of sexual, racial or other minorities; or the elderly and poor. As pervasive as gender differences and inequalities are, they are often hidden – often actively hidden by individuals and institutions acting in what they see as their vested interests, often in collusion with powerful institutional actors such as governments.

Conflicts: Armed conflict is one of the most globally significant drivers of both gender inequality and environmental destruction (Enloe 2016). Globally the pursuit of armed conflict destroys environments, kills and maims uncounted tens of thousands of people, disrupts communities, enhances male privilege and power, and distorts budgets and diverts public finance from social and environmental priorities. The locus of war has moved from battlefields to urban and rural population centres, causing massive migration and creating crises of contaminated water, poor sanitation, inadequate health care, malnourishment, overcrowding and sexual predation in refugee camps (Hynes 2014, Garfield and Neugut 2000).

UNEP has outlined some of the combined effects on gender and environments of conflict situations (UNEP/ UN Women/PBSO/UNDP 2013): women in conflict-affected settings (or even in highly militarized peacetime settings) routinely experience physical insecurity from armed men, including sexual violence, when carrying out daily tasks linked to the collection and use of natural resources; coupled with gender discrimination, conflict-related changes to natural resource access, use and control can significantly increase women's vulnerability and undermine their recovery; land grabs by armed combatants dislocate both women and men, but women have less secure claims with which to resist takeovers, or to reclaim land and resources in the post-conflict period; and failure to recognize the specific natural resource-related challenges and opportunities for women in conflict-affected settings can perpetuate discrimination and exacerbate inequality in the peace-building period.

Absence of gender-disaggregated data: Very few data are collected on gender and environment. What is counted counts; or conversely, if it is not counted it is assumed to not count. In addition to the invisibility of gender dynamics caused by a "household" frame of analysis, there have been disappointingly few efforts to collect gender-disaggregated environmentally related data. New initiatives to improve the availability of gender-disaggregated data are promising but nascent.

Recognizing gender – and beyond

The transformation towards the future we want should benefit all. Inclusiveness enhances effectiveness in all spheres of society. Striking the right balance between living well and living within the Earth's environmental limits will require structural changes in institutions, practices, technologies, policies, lifestyles and thinking. This includes, importantly, recognizing the importance of gender as both a social and environmental category and a force. It will also require moving beyond gender binaries: gender identities do not start or stop with "women" and "men." Many individuals and recognized subcultures live outside this binary. Understanding environmental impacts and agency, and the relationships of cultures to the environment, must start with recognizing gender and then moving further.

References

Enloe, C. 2016. *Globalization and Militarism: Feminists Make the Link*. Rowman and Littlefield, Maryland USA.

Garfield, R.M. and Neugut, A.I. (2000). The Human Consequences of War. In *War and Public Health*. (Eds.) B.S. Levy and V.W. Sidel. American Public Health Association, Washington D.C., 27-38.

Holter, Ø.G. (2014). '"What's in it for Men?" Old Question, New Data', *Men and Masculinities,* 17(5), 515-548.

Hynes, H.P. (2014). The "Invisible Casualty of War": The Environmental Destruction of U.S. Militarism, *Different Takes,* 84.

Inter-Parliamentary Union (2015). Women in national parliaments. [Online] Available at: http://www.ipu.org/wmn-e/classif.htm.

McKinsey and Company (2008). *Women Matter 2: Female Leadership, A Competitive Edge for the Future*. McKinsey and Company, New York.

OECD (2014a) *Social Instructions and Gender Index 2014 Synthesis* Report. OECD, Paris.

Queensland Government (2009). *Gender Analysis Toolkit*. Queensland Government, Brisbane.

UN (1992), Rio Declaration on Environment and Development. UN.

UNDP (2014) *Human development report 2014: Sustaining Human Progress: Reducing Vulnerabilities and Building Resilience.*United Nations Development Programme, New York.

UNEP, UN Women, PBSO and UNDP (2013). *Women and Natural Resources: Unlocking the Peacebuilding Potential*.

UN Women (2015) *Progress of the World's Women 2015-2016: Transforming Economies, Realizing Rights* (978-1-63214-015-9).UN Women, New York.

World Economic Forum (2015). *The Global Gender Gap Report 2015: 10th Anniversary Edition.*World Economic Forum, Cologny/ Geneva.

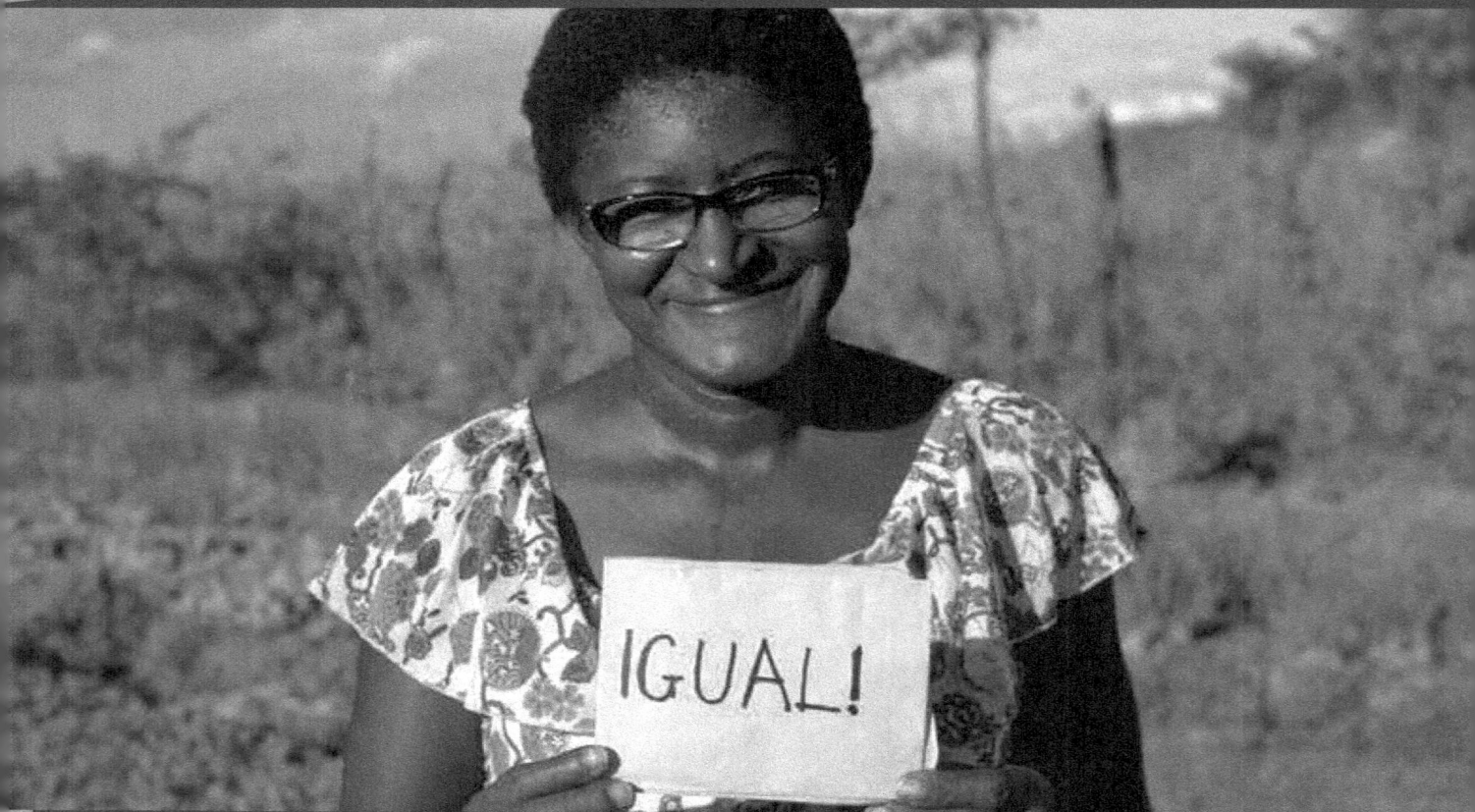

Gender equality cannot be measured by women's or men's presence alone. Participation is not influence; the nature of participation is what makes it meaningful. In the photo: Maria Neida (Brazil) supports the World Bank's "Think Equal" campaign for gender equality.

Photo Credit: © World Bank

CHAPTER

4

Gender equality and sustainable development – connecting the dots

As documented in earlier chapters, gender equality and sustainable development are thoroughly enmeshed. In every assessed environmental dimension – food and energy, or forest and water – it is demonstrably the case that environmental degradation is associated with gender inequalities and in turn also aggravates these inequalities. On the other hand, reducing the gender gap can enable progress towards more sustainable development and environmental solutions.

The primary arguments for enhancing gender equality in environmental policies and actions include:

- Gender equality is a human right with clear benefits for women, but also for men (Fredman and Goldblatt 2015). Most men may not experience the negative effects of gender discrimination at first hand. But they do benefit from a more just society. In particular, men benefit from gender equality in terms of improved health and well-being (Holter 2014).

- Using a "gender lens" to examine environmental policies can make these policies more effective. This approach goes beyond the human rights framework, as it actually promotes gender equality. Nevertheless, use of the gender lens can help achieve progress towards more sustainable development and environmental protection.

- Sustainable development will not advance, nor will environmental protection policies and actions be as effective as they need to be, if gender equality

is not protected and enhanced. Gender equality is a multiplier of sustainability. For example, it strengthens efforts to address poverty and food security. Gender-responsive approaches to problems related to energy, water, sanitation, land and other natural resources are key to protecting human health and the environment.

- If a gender lens is not used, environmental policies may aggravate existing gender inequalities. There are many examples of the introduction of new technologies in the energy and agricultural sectors having unintended inequality-intensifying consequences.

- With the use of an explicit gender lens, environmental policies can contribute to increased gender equality.

- In the absence of a gender lens it is impossible to develop comprehensive assessments of the nature and scale of the most pressing environmental problems.

The world's policy-makers and governments are aware of synergies between gender equality and sustainable development. The outcome document of the 2012 UN Conference on Sustainable Development (Rio+20) acknowledges some of these synergies. In the 2030 Agenda for Sustainable Development, adopted at the UN Sustainable Development Summit in September 2015, countries have made an overarching commitment to realize gender equality (UN 2015). While it is intended that both gender equality and protection of the environment be thoroughly integrated in the 2030 Agenda, only one of the specifically environmental goals actually mentions gender (in fact, "women, youth and local and marginalized communities") (Target 13.b, climate change) and none of the gender-focused goals includes specifically environmental concerns. The continued treatment of these issues in separate "silos" – even to a certain extent in the Sustainable Development Goals (SDGs) – underscores the magnitude of the transformation that is still needed in order to respond adequately to environmental crises.

Countries have the primary responsibility for implementing the 2030 Agenda, together with "all stakeholders". At the national level, implementation of the SDGs is intended to build on existing or emergent legal and policy frameworks. This means countries should either have in place or develop commitments and policy mechanisms to further gender equality and environmental sustainability. In reality, considerable work remains to be done to set the stage for implementing the 2030 Agenda in countries. While the laws of most countries include gender equality provisions, discriminatory legal barriers to women's empowerment and human rights persist; while most countries have environmental protection mechanisms, enforcement is often weak or non-existent. Almost no countries have policy frameworks or mechanisms in place that would enable a synergistic view (let alone implementation) of gender and environmental goals.

Key conclusions

The scarcity of gender-disaggregated data

Environment-related gender-disaggregated data are crucial for gender-and-environment analysis. In all the domains covered by the GGEO, however, gender-disaggregated data are scarce or entirely absent; where available, they are typically fragmented and incomplete, making regional or cross-national comparisons impossible. In some domains, such as the water sector, progress in collecting gender-disaggregated data at the global scale has been reversed. In the absence of gender-disaggregated information, including data, indicators and other information, environmental analyses will be inadequate and partial while establishing realistic baselines, monitoring progress and assessing outcomes will be impossible.

The gender and environment dimension of sustainable development

Unsustainable development activities not only have negative impacts on the environment (including terrestrial and marine ecosystems), but they also create unequal pressures and health consequences for women and men, girls and boys, and vulnerable groups to which they may belong in both developing and developed countries.

Gender boundaries are reflected and defined in economic and productive sectors including energy, fisheries, forestry and livestock production. Activities whose purpose is to end environmentally destructive practices need to be supported by widespread changes in notions about appropriate gender roles.

Narrowing gender gaps in agriculture, water and sanitation, education, research and other areas would increase society's productivity and reduce poverty and hunger appreciably **(Figure 6)**.

Figure 6. The environment affects women and men differently due to gender inequality

Steady progress has been made in access to improved drinking water

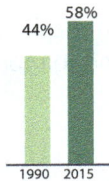

44% 58%

1990 2015

proportion of the population with piped water on premises

Yet, access is low in sub-Saharan Africa and Asia, where women are most often responsible for water collection

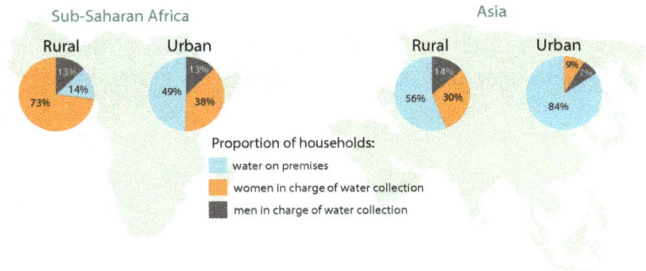

Sub-Saharan Africa

Rural
73% 14% 13%

Urban
49% 38% 13%

Asia

Rural
56% 30% 14%

Urban
84% 9%

Proportion of households:
- water on premises
- women in charge of water collection
- men in charge of water collection

Access to modern energy services has improved

This reduces
1. workload associated with household chores and firewood collection
2. exposure to household air pollution

which affect more women than men

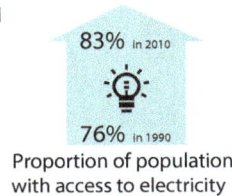

83% in 2010
76% in 1990

Proportion of population with access to electricity

53% in 1990
41% in 2010

Proportion of households using solid fuel for cooking

Gender roles and norms contribute to differences in women's and men's mortality in natural disasters, yet little data are available

2008, cyclone in Myanmar 108,000 deaths

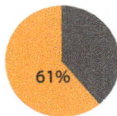

61%

2004, tsunami in Sri Lanka 13,000 deaths

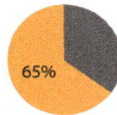

65%

Gender roles and expectations that influence mortality:

Women:
- lower access to information
- lack of swimming skills
- constrained mobility outside their homes

Men:
- risk-taking behaviour
- participation in rescue activities

2004 - 2013, natural disasters in the USA, 5,988 deaths

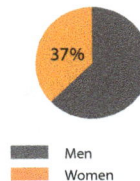

37%

- Men
- Women

Fewer women than men are in decision-making positions

Women account for:

33% of workforce
19% of senior management
} of national meteorological and hydrological services

36% of delegates to the 19th session of the Conference of the Parties to the UN Framework Convention on Climate Change (UNFCCC)

Source: UN (2015b). The World's Women 2015: Trends and Statistics. United Nations, New York.

Consumption patterns are highly gender-differentiated. Reducing the environmental impact of the over-consumption of commodities including cars, cosmetics, meat and plastic products will require shifts in gender-based societal norms that determine the types of consumption and behaviours that are considered acceptable, appropriate or desirable for women and men.

Basic questions about gender and environment cannot be adequately addressed using conventional units of analysis such as "the household" or "the family". Women and men experience "the household" differently and have different authority, resources and control relationships within it.

Women and men play different roles in maintaining livelihoods and well-being at the household and community levels. Understanding their roles as potential agents of change at these levels can indicate pathways to equal opportunities and equal participation in decision-making, which in turn will help ensure more efficient and sustainable natural resources management as well as waste reduction.

Equitable gender and environment policies for the future we want

Until recently, the importance of the gender-and-environment nexus was scarcely recognized. Today there is growing acknowledgement, including in the Sustainable Development Goals (SDGs), that gender and environment are interlinked.

While the importance of the gender-and-environment nexus is increasingly accepted in, for example, international agreements and national policy documents, implementation and follow-through are still largely absent.

A more transformative agenda would call for gender equality as a driver of change, leading to more people-smart environmental policies.

Existing environmental and gender commitments by governments need to be followed up and effectively implemented. Governments have made commitments to gender equality in a number of multilateral environmental agreements and policies, notably the 2030 Agenda and the UN Framework Convention on Climate Change (UNFCCC). To implement those commitments, ensuring gender equality must be understood as more than just counting the number of women participating in a meeting. Real progress is needed at the country level, starting with the integration of gender into national action plans, monitoring and reporting systems, prioritization of the collection and analysis of gender-disaggregated data, and gender budgeting.

Adequate funding and resources will contribute to improvement and progress in developing and implementing gender-sensitive environmental policies. The amount of aid focused on gender equality in fragile states and economies has grown rapidly, but is concentrated in health and education. There is significant under-investment in gender equality in the economic and productive sectors, including agriculture, where women play a major role. This situation could be improved through creating and enabling gender-sensitive financing mechanisms under multilateral environmental agreements and mechanisms such as the

UNFCCC, the Convention to Combat Desertification (UNCCD), the United Nations collaborative initiative on Reducing Emissions from Deforestation and forest Degradation in developing countries (REDD+), the Basel, Stockholm and Rotterdam Conventions, the Convention on Biological Diversity, Climate Investment Funds (CIFs), the Global Environment Facility (GEF) and the Global Climate Fund (GCF).

Gender-sensitive environmental assessments are needed at national and international levels. Environmental assessment tools (e.g. environmental impact assessments and strategic environmental assessments) and safeguard measures, which may be required as a prerequisite for development plans and activities, need to take gender aspects into account. This could be done through making gender impact assessments (GIAs) mandatory in public and private environmental reviews and permitting, licensing and planning activities. Conducting national-level "state of gender and the environment" assessments would help establish a baseline context against which future changes and progress might be measured. International support to carry out these activities would need to be provided to developing countries.

Gender-disaggregated information is essential. Strengthening the focus on developing, collecting and analysing gender-disaggregated data, indicators and other information (including at the intra-household level) would support more effective environmental decision-making. This would include efforts to "lift the roof off the household" in data collection, revealing intra-household gender relations, assets and roles in resource utilization and decision-making. It is necessary to move beyond gender binaries and use a wider lens

in regard to social-environmental relations. The value of qualitative information, which is especially valuable in capturing intra-household dynamics, should be recognized and brought into official data streams to support in-depth understanding of the complexity of social dynamics, especially where quantitative data are missing or too costly to obtain. It is also important to promote and support the development of gender-disaggregated environment-related indicators with respect to the implementation of the Sustainable Development Goals (SDGs) at national and subnational levels.

It is essential to promote and support women's voices, leadership and organization. The science, technology, engineering and math (STEM) disciplines are particularly important in environmental management and in promoting gender equality along the environmental and science expertise pipeline, but they are highly gender unbalanced. Gender equality also needs to be addressed in the agricultural extension, forestry, water management and technical advisory fields, as well as in wildlife management, parks conservation and management, and training to carry out environmental and strategic impact assessments.

In addition, diverse voices need to be brought into formal environmental governance systems, and strong goals should be established for achieving gender equality in governance at the local through the national and multilateral levels. Integrating environmental issues into existing national gender policies, as well as providing capacity building for existing and emergent civil society organizations (including women's, indigenous and youth groups) on environmental sustainability and sustainable development would reinforce gender-and-environment links, as well as meaningful participation in environmental decision-making and programme implementation **(Figure 7)**.

It is important to bring men and boys, as well as women and girls, into the gender-and-environment conversation. Everyone benefits from sustainable environmental development. Gender equality benefits men, boys, and people who gender-identify as male; some of these people, as well as women, girls and people who gender-identify as female, warrant special attention as they strive to overcome a past and present of discrimination. Creating a safe, healthy and equitable future that leaves no one behind is the responsibility of all, and can be of benefit to all.

Enabling conditions for large-scale transformations with respect to the environment and gender need to be created. Large-scale socio-economic structures and policies have both positive and negative effects on the environment and on gender equality. Leveraging positive effects while minimizing negative ones is challenging, but can provide opportunities to create enabling environments in which social equality, inclusiveness and well-being are combined with environmental sustainability. It is essential to develop policies that prioritize social well-being over individual and short-term economic gains.

Issues of unpaid work and time poverty need to be addressed. Both women and men perform "care economy" functions. Women's share of such work is usually larger and is often unrecognized, encompassing not only child rearing and home care but also invisible production activities. Recognizing the contributions of people who take care of families and communities, as well as those who perform subsistence agricultural and other work, would make it possible to account more fully for the value of this work; to address time poverty issues; to increase capacities to redistribute paid and unpaid work within households, among households, and between households and governments; and thus to consider the care economy and unpaid work in initiatives aimed at achieving sustainable development and gender justice.

Figure 7: Heads of national environmental sector ministries in UN Member States (women and men) in 2015

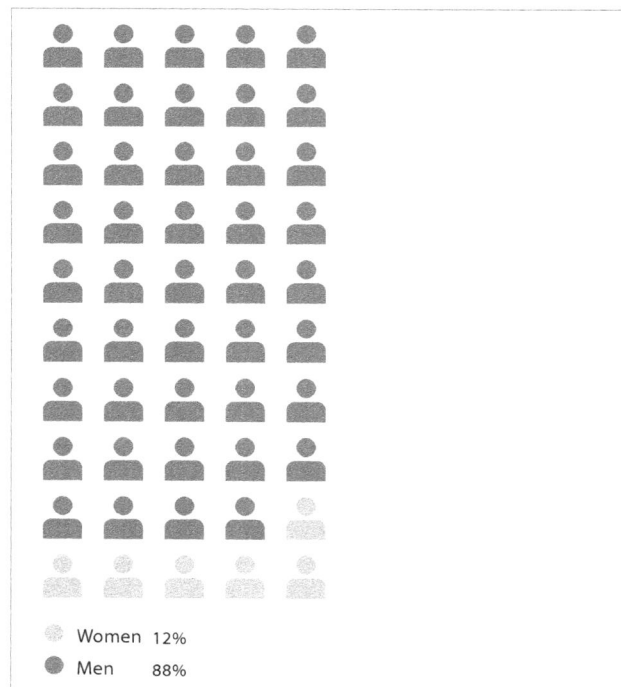

Women 12%
Men 88%

Source: IUCN (2015)

References

Fredman, S. and Goldblatt, B. (2015). *For Progress of the World's Women 2015-2016: Gender Equality and Human Rights*. UN Women, New York.

Holter, Ø.G. (2014). „What's in it for Men?" Old Question, New Data, *Men and Masculinities,* 17(5), 515-548.

IUCN (2015). Women's Participation in Global Environmental Decision Making: *New research from the Environment and Gender Index* (EGI). IUCN, Washington D.C.

UN (2015). *Transforming Our World: The 2030 Agenda for Sustainable Development.* United Nations.

UN (2015b). T*he World's Women 2015: Trends and Statistics.*United Nations, New York.

www.ingramcontent.com/pod-product-compliance
Lightning Source LLC
Chambersburg PA
CBHW080001280326
41935CB00013B/1711